Testimonials
(Advance Praise)

"Stability, The Belle of the Ball, has an excellent opening that immediately captures the reader's interest. Perfect! Marie, you are truly an amazing woman! Coming from Haiti, and all its challenges you have created a wonderful life for you and yours! It is an Honor to be your Friend!"

—H. Douglas Thornley,
Former President,
Impact Colors

"Stability, The Belle of the Ball, is intriguing from the start. I admire this young girl's effort and determination. What a way to bring Haiti's culture to the front of the line."

—Tom Branna,
VP/Editorial Director,
Happi/Rodman Media

"An in-depth look of the motivation behind emigration and the reason why people leave their homeland are well represented in *Stability, The Belle of the Ball.*"

—Brenda (Payne) Whiteman,
Author and Fulfillment and Review Writer,
Food for the Poor (FFTP)

"The story is fascinating. It makes me appreciate others [sic] struggle even more."

—**Giorgio Dell'Acqua,**
PhD, Chief Science Officer,
Nutrafol, a Unilever Company

"Very beautifully written and touching. Written straight from the heart."

—**Gerard Viegas,**
Managing Partner,
NurseLadder.com

"I see a love story and the clashing of two worlds between the parents of a young teenager."

—**Thalia Thomas,**
MPA, MSN, CCM, RN, Case Manager,
RWJ Barnabas Health

"The opening scene is compelling and interesting. I enjoy it when there is a bit of a tease that is circled back to later. It sets the tone and makes the reader want to learn more. I feel like [sic] I am watching a movie at times, and other times I feel like [sic] I'm speaking with a friend."

—**Jennifer Amato,**
Content Coordinator,
Best Version Media

Stability

The Belle of the Ball

Stability

The Belle of the Ball

Marie Renée Thadal
with the assistance of Susan Torres

Halo
PUBLISHING
INTERNATIONAL

Halo
PUBLISHING
INTERNATIONAL

Halo Publishing International
7550 WIH-10 #800, PMB 2069,
San Antonio, TX 78229

First Edition, November 2023
ISBN: 978-1-63765-407-1
Library of Congress Control Number: 2023908885

Stability, The Belle of the Ball, is dedicated to my revolutionary ancestors whose genes I carry; to my grandparents who were eminent leaders in their farming village; to my uncle Jean, the real VIP, whose bravery and charisma led him to America; to my darling father, Joe, who understood family devotion and followed his brother to the new country, but had the heart to look back; to my children for enhancing my purpose in life; and last, but not least, to my mother who put it all on the line to win it all.

Also, to my loving brothers for being my rock, to the neighbors and other good souls who watched over me, to every teacher and professor who infused me with knowledge, to my cousins and every family member who blessed me with unconditional love, to the two mothers who subbed as my mom when I was separated from my biological mother, to my dearest friends who have treated me more like family than friends, to my amazing colleagues at my company and management team for allowing me to blossom and assume my leadership position in the cosmetics industry, to the board members and volunteers of the Society of Cosmetic Chemists for teaching me how to work for the greater good, to the volunteers and supporters of Itiah Angels for Learning, nonprofit organization for demonstrating your exceptional love for humankind and those in need. Every single one of you provided a piece of the puzzle of my life that made me the person I am today. For that, I cherish you.

Contents

Introduction

This work is a memoir. It reflects the author's present recollections of her experiences over a period of years. Certain names, locations, and identifying characteristics may have been changed. Dialogue and events have been recreated from memory and, in some cases, have been compressed to convey the substance of what was said or what occurred.

Chapter 1

The Land of Opportunity

Leave It All Behind

His simple words rang in my head, *"TiFoune,*[1] *I will see you soon. I will send for you one day, my little girl. Be good to your mother, listen to her, and continue to do well in school."*

I never understood what "one day" meant, but I held on to his words as one accepts a polite goodbye.

Named Joseph René at birth, my father promptly became Joe when he left his homeland. A native of Haiti, he was of small stature and had deep-velvet, dark skin, and a determined heart. He was born and raised in the beautiful mountains of Trouin[2]—a town in the western side of Haiti, south of the capital city of Port-Au-Prince—where, behind each mountain peak, there is another mountain peak to climb, according to the Haitian Creole proverb *"Dèyè mòn, gen mòn."* The discovery of nature and the secrets behind each mountain are endless.

Joe helped on his parents' farm, but stored a hopeful dream in his mind of voyaging from his birthplace to the capital city to continue his education. In the mountains, children expect their education to cease with primary-school completion at about the age of thirteen. Working on the farm, in many cases, takes precedence over gaining an education, but Joe was determined to learn in his own way. As soon as he had the chance, he ventured away from farm life and left his humble home while he was in his twenties.

A consummate enthusiast, he traveled to Port-Au-Prince and found lodging with a group of sisters who were missionaries from France. With an aptitude for fixing electronics, cars, and anything mechanical, he discovered his niche and found paid work in the city. Realizing that his mechanical skills made him worthy of being employable, he found himself in a category of those who were in a promising economic class.

Meeting my mother, Aline, brought life into my father's world. My mother's family was of the elite class of Haiti who had the opportunity to travel back and forth to Cuba, where she was born. This one difference seeped into their love relationship. Adding to this, her distinctive appearance—fair, cocoa-brown complexion and brown hair with shades of auburn—turned heads wherever they roamed.

Initially, Joe's attachment was possessive because of what my mother was made of, and his doubtful mind released waves of insecurities. I think he believed that he could lose her at any time. And for a Haitian, manhood is the spine that holds one upright; his feelings of being less than would eventually cause disturbance in their relationship. But in the end, they somehow found each other in the same community, opened their hearts to romance, each blooming like beds of pansies, and succumbed to love. Since their connection appeared to have a sense of ease, they became a couple hoping to encounter everlasting happiness.

Joe and Aline settled in a type of home commonplace in Haiti: small, but with the necessities for eating, sleeping, and fostering a community. Soon after, I was born, the only girl in the family. My mother already had two sons, Max and Yves-Antoine, so she was undoubtedly delighted when I was born, as having a daughter is a security she would need in her old age. Max was nearly twenty years old when I was born, and he lived in another residence close to the secondary school he attended. But Yves-Antoine, ten years older than I, was still living at home. He was not happy since he was expecting a baby brother whom he could teach how to play *fútbol*.

With the family's needs growing, our home life became stressed with economic strain. So as the leader of the family, my father knew what he had to do: find lucrative ways to support us, even if this meant leaving the family and his homeland, Haiti.

The night before he left, my mother told us what to expect. I knew what she was about to say to us, as I had heard bits and pieces of their whispering conversations for months, but it seemed too far-fetched.

"We need money to raise the kids. More importantly, their education is of utmost priority, and America has many jobs. After all, it's the land of opportunity," a hoarse whispering voice would say.

"I know, I know," my mother's supportive response would repeatedly chant.

I heard different versions for months, but I couldn't quite envision my father hurrying off to an unknown land. But even as a nine-year-old, I knew he was up to something; he was like that, a man of his own making.

It was a typical day on a scorching Saturday afternoon, but playing outside with my neighborhood friends made any weather discomfort nonexistent. I was practicing my rope-jumping routine while singing a favorite song. With the enthusiasm of a carefree child who harnessed happiness as if this state of being personally belonged to me, I didn't realize my life was about to be changed forever.

As a child growing up on the island of Haiti, I had no worries. Life was sweet and simple, as every child's life should be. I adored my mother and admired my father, even though his presence made me anxious sometimes. We would scatter like scared mice when his frustrations blackened the room. As the family's patriarch, he was also angered by all that he could not provide for the family.

The Haitian culture was tight-knit with warmth and pride; small communities were like that, looking out for each other's kids and planning casual gatherings to pass the time. Haiti was my homeland, and I had never thought of leaving it. My childhood days were all connected, from one day to the next and the next. I had no complaints.

"TiFoune, TiFoune, we need to talk about some important news. Come here; come inside."

Close to the doorway, outside of our home, my friends and I were joyfully playing, jumping rope, dancing, and singing to the sound of the radio playing *chansonettes françaises*.[3] I quickly stopped, dropped the rope, and ran towards the door. I always tried to obey my mother immediately when she called, especially when there was usually a leather object dangling on a nearby hook to remind everyone of its job—it kept us in line.

When I entered the shared family room, my father was at the far end in a corner. Sitting on the wooden family stool with his hands clasped together, resting on his lap, and his head slightly lowered, he was eyeing the ground with intensity as if he was concentrating on his inner voice. My mother was standing in the center of the room and had all the tell-tale signs of a person prepping for a memorable speech—back and chin upright, lips partly open, and hands folded behind her. I felt the thickness in the air when I walked into the room. I knew a critical conversation was about to occur.

My brother Yves-Antoine came in the room, right behind me, catching his breath. After eyeing my parents, he sat on the small divan in the center of the room, plopping down next to me.

When my mother opened her mouth to speak, I wanted to blurt out questions, but dared not interrupt. Finally, I couldn't withhold my curiosity. "Are we taking a trip to Grandma and Grandpa's farm in Trouin? When are we going?"

My mother often added dramatic flair when announcing we were planning to take a trip, so I just assumed that was the business of the day.

"No, it's not about that."

"Did Yves-Antoine's teacher send a note home again? Is he getting another punishment?"

"No, no. It's about Father. He must go."

"Go where?" By the look on her face, it didn't seem disappointing news, so I waited patiently for more of an explanation.

"Your father will go to America to live with Uncle Jean," she stated with a serious and regal tone, then paused, looked over at my father, and finished, "and to find work."

"Will all of us go too? Yay! We are going to America!"

"No, no, no. He is going by himself."

Our enthusiasm was suddenly stifled. Then my father slowly stood up from the stool, walked over to our circle, looked over our curious heads, and broke his silence to address us like a military leader, "I will go to America to work, and all of you will stay. Work is good over there, so I must go. But do not worry. I will work with one purpose—to have all of you by my side."

His eyes met mine for a brief moment; then he looked over at my mother, and his crooked smile matched hers. Both were our parents, but at that moment, they were more than parents; they were change agents who were about to transform our family legacy.

The mood in the air was paralyzing for a few seconds, and then exhilaration filled the room like a tidal wave of newfound inspiration. I ran over to my father and hugged half of his torso so tight that I felt his breath gasp. Part of me was aware that there was reason to celebrate. Anyone who left Haiti to settle in America advanced their lives. Haitians often dreamed of a way out of poverty and despair, and this was an opportunity for my father. My mother and brother were beaming in the background as if they were leaving, too.

When I look back, I didn't know it then, but my father was also planning my future. His personal journey would eventually connect to mine.

Within just a few weeks, his departure was set. It was challenging to keep this family secret from the neighbors and my best friend, Gina. But it was an order from my father that we had to obey. We lived in a survival climate and needed to protect our dreams, whether for superstitious reasons or against actual harm.

One Sunday, before the baby birds would welcome the new day, my father left. The entire town was deep in sleep, but not I. I heard my mother whisper some final affectionate words, then a soft goodbye. I heard the squeak of the door's opening. I heard the gentle closing of the door. I heard my heart pounding in my chest.

Fathers in Haiti commonly leave the family home to find work elsewhere so they can send money to support the household from afar. It is a practice that leaves most homes with one parent—often the mother—to be the family's leader. This is a responsibility held by the highest power.

The other option is to send a child to live with another family. This is a common practice known as *rest avek*,[4] but child labor and abuse are more predictably the lives led by these children. Even if abuse is not involved, the child under this arrangement is expected to provide maid services during the day, in exchange for night-school privileges arranged by the new family. Many families choose this option as a last resort, so it was a relief that neither my brother nor I would be sent away.

After all, this time Father wasn't just going to another city to work. He was going to America! It was an unexpected blessing that fell upon our humble family. This opportunity was a long time coming, and my father's younger brother was the catalyst for this life-changing move. From this experience alone, I was taught that families who link their chains of support together have more power than those who do it alone.

My father's adventurous younger brother, Jean, left his hometown of Trouin a few years before my father. A happenstance on a cruise line led him to America. He had secured a position on a ship, which was a challenging task. While on the ship, Uncle Jean met a group of parishioners from an Episcopalian church, and he mentioned that our family in Haiti also were Episcopalians. They all listened as my uncle described the tiny white building, Saint Mathias Church, by the roadside where the village folks gathered every Sunday to worship. The church was about a mile away from my grandparents' hut. It also housed the only primary school in the village.

Throughout the cruise, the parishioners grew closer to Uncle Jean, and in return, he made sure they enjoyed their vacation and showered them with exceptional service. Lo and behold, before the week ended, Uncle Jean was invited to visit their church in Princeton, New Jersey. He had docked in Miami and was familiar with other cities in the United States that he had heard of, but Uncle Jean was often inclined to greet adventure and was known for his whimsical ways. So he accepted this invitation in good faith. In no time, the church members organized all the necessary documents with Immigration Services so Uncle Jean could legally reside in America.

Uncle Jean settled in Princeton, New Jersey, and within months, secured employment and had a place he could call home. Alone in America and longing for his family, he reached out to his parents and siblings in Haiti and promised them he would work hard on sponsoring them.

This singular turn of events introduced an opportunity for my father to come to America. So with blind faith, he decided to leave Haiti to join his brother and dare to chase the American dream. After arriving in the United States, my father began working as a custodian at a local hospital. He didn't like the work, but he accepted his fate. An hourly wage suited him. He worked tirelessly and soon began to send money to my mother monthly. Life in Haiti improved for all of us.

Back in Haiti, my oldest brother, Max, and his wife found themselves in a precarious political situation under the Duvalier dictatorship's regime. Francois Duvalier, also known as Papa Doc, was the president of Haiti who ruled from 1957 to 1971. My brother's involvement in politics became very risky for his family, and he was forced to leave his two young daughters with my mother. This caused additional financial strain on my family, so having a family member, such as my father, work outside of Haiti in America and send money back home was a lifesaver for us. The dream of escaping generational poverty was now within our family's reach.

In time, I learned from my mother that my father decided to pursue a trade and attend a vocational school. He warned that money from him would be scarce. He longed to exceed beyond what he was born into, and he needed to advance from his current position. I so respected him for this. Though he would have wanted to attend a university to achieve a degree in mechanical engineering, a trade school was the practical option. As a young girl, the idea of my father living across the seas and securing a profession in America granted me permission to dream outside the walls of what my little country offered.

Months passed, and life went back to normal—the same routine, hour by hour, minute by minute—different days, but everything else the same, over and over again. Nothing much shifted, but the breeze in the wind, until one day a large yellow package arrived from my father.

Unsure of what she was about to read, my mother carefully tore open the top of the envelope and then paused. "TiFoune, TiFoune, go get your brother. He's playing fútbol with the boys in the field. Tell him to come here now!"

When I returned with my brother, who was huffing and puffing, my mother was reading the letter. Her eyes and mouth widened, and a yelp escaped her lungs. She spread pictures and documents on the table, showcasing my father's accomplishments. A copy of my father's diploma from the trade school and photographs of him in his glory brought us all a state of joy. We huddled close to my mother to draw in all our eyes could read and see. My father was the first in his graduating class at the trade school and was also awarded for perfect attendance.

Our faces beamed with happiness. Still, we knew better than to show others our newfound success, for fear they would become envious and eventually resent our family. This was the unspoken rule, so we quietly celebrated with pride. My father's accomplishment was ours too; it was shared and owned by all of us.

The letter explained that, on the day of his graduation, with his diploma in hand, my father confidently entered the office of Mercer Metro Bus Company in Trenton, which later became called New Jersey Transit. I recalled the words he would utter repeatedly in the coming years, "They hired me on the spot as a lead mechanic; this has never been done before at the company." Joe was a proud Haitian man.

Money became more consistent after his hire, and our family life had a sacred kind of security. We had enough of what was needed, but only just enough.

Chapter 2
Life without Father

The Cards You Are Dealt

With Papa absent from the home, our living conditions required some adjustments, so we moved into what is known as *lakou dis pieces*.[5] This community-housing development consisted of individual, oversized rooms that included an enclosed patio for cooking. My mother thought living in this community supported our family's needs since my father was gone.

In our new place, we had six people in one room—my mother, my brother Yves-Antoine, my brother Max's two daughters, a family friend, and me. We slept on two queen-sized mattresses stacked on top of each other during the day, then separated and laid them out on the floor each evening. My brother had his twin-size bed on the opposite side of the room. The family friend slept on the floor at the foot of the bed. She dutifully cooked and cleaned for us to earn her right to have a place to sleep each night. We shared the latrine, showers, and running water with the entire community of ten different families.

Living under these conditions was everyone's normal. A simple yet hard life. The row of houses was situated near a brick-making lot that functioned during the day. When the workday ended, children of the lakou *dis pieces* used this empty lot for playing hopscotch, jumping rope, and tackling each other in fútbol.

As a close-knit group of people, we led a routine life. Kids watched crowds of people and cars go by as entertainment in the evening. Some days, *raconteurs*[6] shared sorcery and ghost stories with the children. This type of storytelling was terrifying for little children, but it served a twisted purpose; it kept us from roaming away from home, especially after dark.

Caring families watched out for each other's kids and often doled out life lessons as they came up. We all got along, except when the neighbor's daughter quarreled with the wife of the commandant in Duvalier's army. Later that day, an army truckful of *gendarmes*—armed police officers sporting black shades to hide their identities—arrived and took her to prison. Scenes like this terrified me. In those times, life without a father at home felt insecure.

On two other occasions, I had similar fearful feelings. At the end of each school year, radio announcements were made naming the students who passed the *Certificat*[7] exam to be promoted from primary to secondary school.

Neighbors anxiously gather around the radio to hear whose names were going to be called. Sitting with my neighbors on sturdy wooden benches surrounding the radio, anticipating favorable news from the school board, it was as if we were waiting to hear the winning lottery numbers. And, really, that is precisely what it was. Depending on the results, students were either glorified winners or unfortunate losers.

Alongside my mother, I sat with the crowd looking intently at this box with speakers that would predict the future of my education. The radio announcer's voice was robotic, but melodic; you almost wanted to dance to it. The school official began the declaration in formal French, Haiti's official language. The names were called in alphabetical order as students impatiently and nervously waited. Each time students in our group heard their names, there was a soft celebration.

My family and I listened attentively. Finally, "Michaud, Marie Renée," my given name, was announced. We all gasped for air; everyone hugged me, but we quickly regained our composure and dutifully sat down to hear more names called.

On another occasion, my mother attended the distribution of report cards at my school.

"Now we will inform all the parents of the students' efforts this past semester. The grades prove that your children studied very hard, and you know that effort is always rewarded by passing grades. So I would like to deliver the most important announcement first—the student who is first in the class."

The school's headmistress, a holy sister, paused for a few seconds, but it seemed like minutes. There was a stillness in the air. I could hear faint breathing in the room, but nothing else, not even outside noise from the streets. *Or did time stop?* I remembered thinking. I clasped my hands on my lap to hold in any reaction that would prematurely sprout out of my body.

Sister's voice resumed, "I am proud to announce that Marie Renée Michaud is the top student for this marking period!"

My heart pounded with excitement and youthful pride, but I was also fearful of how I would be treated going forward. My eyes tentatively peered around the room to read the reactions of other mothers and family members. Their awkward smiles said it all. I was the competition now.

Then I locked eyes with my mother. Her happiness meant everything to me; I wanted to excel for both of us. She held back her verbal emotions as I walked back towards her with my report card in hand, but her face was fashioned with a controlled smile full of joy she could not hide. "*TiFoune,* congratulations! I am so proud of you! That's my girl," she whispered in my ear and wrapped one arm around my shoulders to give me a mildly tight hug.

I held in the excitement, but my face wanted to betray me. My eyes widened outside the normal bounds, my teeth clenched when I grinned, and my hands joined my mother's as we squeezed them together. My inner pride was an asset that I nurtured without knowing that I did, and support from my mother kept this in place as I sensed her faith in me, even as a young child. We were a team, growing together harmoniously. My father would be proud.

My academic record was always solid and steady. My mother was secretly proud during that marking period when I finished at the top of my class. I say secretly because the community didn't openly embrace the success of others at times. The competition was fierce. When one student excelled over another, it was more like a threat. My mother knew how to carefully shield and position her motherly glee; she behaved humbly, surprised when my name was announced.

I remember that day well. Only my mother's closest friends heard the stories of how she shielded me from any potentially evil-intentioned parents, and how she needed to protect her only daughter. "You should have seen me," she told her friends. "I could have won a medal for best actress," she continued with a smile on her face. "I played the part of the surprised mother so well."

Achieving academic success was a family aspiration in most Haitian households. More so because there was a lot riding on the outcome. Receiving an education offered the promise of economic transformation for the student and the entire family. On the downside, when a student failed, they were guaranteed a *teebood*—a shameful whip-ping—when they got home for disappointing their family. On one occasion, I received my dose of discipline from my father for being third in the class; I'd sooner forget that spanking, but that was the way children were kept in line.

Failing classes was the first offense, and wasting hard-earned money was the second. A child who had to repeat a grade caused additional expenses for the family because summer classes were required. This was a severe financial hardship and an embarrassment for everyone involved. If the child continued to fail, a family decision was enforced. The child would either discontinue their formal education, attend night school, or find a trade outside of academia altogether.

For the females, getting married was an option that relieved them from the responsibility of pursuing an education, so their vocation would ultimately fall under the title of wife and mother. Fortunately, my mother understood the possibilities an education would bring to one's life, so she provided me with the support and every resource that I needed for my schooling.

Attending school in Haiti meant sacrifices: monetary and lifestyle inconveniences. Traveling to school alone was a monumental quest, especially if you didn't have the means to travel by private car or pay for public transportation. While a few students were privileged with car rides, it took me nearly an hour to walk each way, mainly in the brutal and beating hot sun. My brother willingly escorted me each and every day and never complained, even though his school was very close to our home. This was the way in our family. We connected, we sacrificed, and we grew alongside each other.

Wearing uniforms to school was mandatory. I remember observing the pristine fabric of other students' uniforms.

Though they were exactly the same—a white blouse with white buttons around the waist attached to a navy-blue skirt—some differed from mine. At times I marveled at the quality material and how they seemed to have the smoothness and thickness of luxury. Those same children also had money to buy extravagant lunches from the local bakery near the school. I learned early in life who had and who didn't, and knew which category I was closer to. My inner drive to want better, more, or different than what I was born into rumbled in my heart, yearning for equality and justice.

Haiti, for me, was just a place in time as I waited for my father's call from America. And when it came, it was like a sudden burst of sunshine after a torrential rain.

Chapter 3
Transitions in Motion

Walking into our one-room home from school, I noticed my mother sitting on the wooden family stool. Her gaze was defiant. Her lips were pursed. Her back was military straight. Knowing my mother's body language, she had something to tell me that would impact my day.

So after I placed my books on the nearby table, I decided to prod into her thinking. "Mama, school was grueling today. The teacher called on me to recite word for word the chapters in my history book about the life of the one and only king of Haiti, Henry Christophe, and then I recited it just as I was taught: '...who after the revolution pro- claimed himself King Henry the First...'!"

His story is a fascinating one. After all, he was a former slave who became quite a distinguished leader during the Haitian Revolution. His legacy is marked by the mas- sive fortress known as the Citadelle Laferriere, which is located in North Haiti.

"Regurgitating our lessons word for word is so boring! Instead of memorizing and reciting, I wish we could do a play on the life of the presidents," I continued. This was one of my pretty common complaints about school. "Wouldn't that be great, Mama?"

She didn't respond.

"And also, I noticed my uniform is not like those of the other girls, Mama. Their skirt fabric looks very pretty! I wish I could get that kind, Mama. But, anyway, mine is always well ironed, right?"

Finally, awakening from her silence, my mother spoke, "*TiFoune*, could you please go get me a glass of water?"

Immediately, I ran out the door to get the water. I took a glass and walked four units toward the back of the community, where the water spigot was located, which supplied water to the entire block. When I came back, my mother was slowly pacing in our small space.

She reached out for the glass of water, took a sip, then gradually placed it on the table. "*TiFoune*, I need to talk to you. I have to tell you something important, very important."

"Yes, Mama. What is it? Tell me!"

"We need to talk about your father."

"What do you mean? Is he okay? Mama, tell me, tell me!!"

"No, he's fine. Don't worry, my little girl."

"Then what?"

"It's time that you join him."

"What? Really? In America?"

"Yes, he will send the petition papers to the embassy, and you will soon go to live with him."

"That's so, so exciting! Finally, we are going to be with Papa! Wait…just me? Am I leaving you? Mama, is that okay?"

"Yes, this is something good for you. Your father is making good on his promise. You see, you will have it much better in America, much better."

"Well, this is great. I get to see Papa again. He's been gone forever! But what about you, Mama?"

Then her motherly warmth surfaced, and she drew closer to me. *"TiFoune, TiFoune,* my lovely baby girl"—she cupped my face in her soft, graceful hands—"I will miss you so, so much. We will speak on the phone, I promise. When the money comes, I will go to the *Teleco* company and call you. We will write to each other all the time, too. I love you. I love you, little girl of mine."

I noted inside my mind that I would miss that sense of belonging to my mother and the words of endearment that only we shared. Then I nodded in response, holding back adolescent tears for as long as I could. But the corners of my mouth turned downwards, and large, stored droplets of tears spilled out of my eyes unexpectedly. Tears of impending homesickness and tears of unknown joy ahead. We hugged and hugged tightly.

My mother was teary-eyed, but not sobbing; she released her emotions as I did. Then we both stopped our crying session, gazed into each other's eyes, and smiled. The day my father left, I had the same feelings. I would miss him, but I knew it was all for the best. Haiti was my homeland, my place of birth, and no country, near or far, could change that fact. Whether the unfortunate poverty damaged its reputation of being an ideal place to come from or not, it was still my first humble home, where my soul seeds were planted.

"Go get your brother. You can tell him the news, but no one else in the neighborhood should know at this time. The younger nieces should not know either. They might blurt it out. It is our big, big secret."

Preparations for sending me to America began immediately. We were excited, and the anticipation of my leaving hung in the air as if it were a life-or-death event. In a way, it was. My family in Haiti could continue to live in educational deficiency and generational poverty, or we could cross over traditional lines and transform the family legacy for the better.

With transitions in motion, I followed along. When my father's petition was finally approved, we went to the United States Embassy for the interview, only to be disappointed. My visa was denied.

As it turned out, my birth certificate recorded my father's name as Joseph René, while all his vital papers had him as Joseph Serené. This discovery caused a road-block and shattered our plan—we were stripped of hope. My journey to America might not happen. My mother didn't know where to turn or how to investigate why this faulty naming occurred.

But my mother was determined to carry out this mission of getting my visa. It would be one long, arduous year and many visits to the United States Embassy in Port-Au-Prince before my petition was finally approved.

As we later learned from my grandfather, when they asked my grandmother to state the name of her baby boy, she verbally responded, "*Se* René," meaning, "It's René." The word "se" means "it is." We learned that the person recording the information for my father's birth certificate must have misunderstood and thought the "se" was part of his name, not part of a sentence, so the name that was recorded was *Se*rené. I am not sure how Mama managed to legally revise my birth certificate with my father's real name, but it was successfully executed. To say it was a monumental victory is putting it lightly.

Haitians often refer to themselves as *les grands noirs*, the magnificent Blacks, *who renounced the life of captivity and oppression*. After all, Haitians were the first group of enslaved Blacks to fight and win their independence from slavery, and become the first Black republic. "Live free or die" was their guiding principle. But liberty comes at a cost. For centuries, Haiti has suffered abuse from other countries, corruption by its own government, and treacherous weather conditions, as well as natural disasters of all types. With constant political unrest and the exodus of its highly educated citizens, the Pearl of the Antilles has become one of the poorest countries in the Western Hemisphere. Such extreme poverty has forced Haitians to embrace their strengths and harbor resilience to deal with these unsettling circumstances.

Knowing that change was on the horizon, my entire family quietly celebrated as we waited for my father to send money to purchase my plane tickets. He decided that it was best to coordinate the date with my grandparents, who were accustomed to traveling back and forth to New Jersey, and other family members who were planning to travel on the same day.

At last, Mama came to me with the biggest smile and shared that the date was set, and I would leave Haiti. I concealed my nervousness, knowing it was the opportunity of a lifetime to go to America. Leaving behind my mother and family members felt as if I had a new life arrangement with a secret motive—beating the odds. It was as though I were the conduit for familial success. I was a magnificent *Black*, and I would leave Haiti with a firm grip on my feelings and identity. A few uncontrollable tears escaped down my young cheeks, but mostly my emotions were dressed in maturity and prideful strength. When Haitians travel away from their homeland, they take their *grand-noir* attitude with them. It's in our Haitian bloodlines, and I desperately wanted to live up to my prideful heritage.

When I laid my head down to sleep at night, my thoughts whirled as if it were a movie reel going in fast-forward motion. Questions danced frantically in my head. *Where is my life taking me? What will this new country be like? Will there be any young people like me, and will they speak French or perhaps Creole?* Then there was the fact that I was leaving my family and going to live with my father, the man I no longer knew. Emotionally, I struggled with breathing it all in, but this is where the audacity to use this opportunity directed my thinking. I would soldier on and accept my adventure; I was prepared to leave my home on Center Street. It was time to move away, to a country where pursuing an education changed lives.

Several weeks after my mother proclaimed a new life for me, a car with Laina, my uncle Jean's sister-in-law; Loileau, a family friend; and my paternal grandparents came to take me to the airport. Information about my departure was held within the family circle until the final hour. The news of my leaving wasn't shared among the community because my mother feared that others would harm me. So on the day of my departure, only my mother, brother, two nieces, and close neighbors gathered in front of my house and waited with me.

I stood next to two valises, one on each side, as if they were my only companions. Inside my suitcases were a few brand-new outfits for my brand-new life. I wore a cream-colored polyester pants suit (my first time wearing pants), and my curly hair was straightened and coiffed by a hairdresser the night before. I was rolling with style. I felt ready on the outside, but on the inside, my thoughts were scrambling for emotional rest.

As soon as the car pulled up, I experienced a jolt of hurried anxiety. Everything was happening so fast. Turning to my brother and neighbors, I offered them individual hugs. I grabbed one valise, and my brother took the other one to put in the car trunk; then I gave him an extra-long hug. My mother and I got in the car because she planned to see me off. I sat in the car's back seat, then quickly turned my head to see everyone smiling and waving their hands. That sight soon faded.

We passed Saint Anne's Square. We passed my favorite bakery and the church where I was baptized; we passed my best friend's home. I was leaving behind my childhood neighborhood, the shared shower rooms and latrine, and the long, winding roads leading to my school. Saying goodbye to *lakou dis pieces* felt as if I were saying goodbye to a part of my life that I would never return to again. I, Marie Renée, was on my way to America to start a new life.

Between my grandparents and my mother, I was surrounded by excitable, noisy adults who were endlessly chattering in Creole. At the same time, I sat spellbound and stared out the window, knowing something life-changing was happening. I was leaving Haiti, my family, my friends, and all that I knew. When these thoughts chimed in,

I felt confused, slightly guilty, then indifferent. Quickly, I readjusted my thinking and thought of my determined father, who was waiting for me. I conveniently shoved the thoughts of my home and all of its memories inward. I vowed to become that *magnificent Black,* the strong, resilient native Haitian who would improve the next generation.

It was later explained to me that I was only able to reconnect with my father because of the US Family Unification immigration policy instituted in the 1960s. At the time, I didn't realize how fortunate I was and how my father had set me on the right path.

The drop-off was just as quick as the pickup. Fortunately, I wasn't alone. Having the small party of family members and friends traveling with me felt comforting. We were Haitians on a mission. When we arrived at the airport, we pulled up alongside the entrance, exited one by one, and then the driver settled the valises on the sidewalk and sped away.

My mother stood still, bracing for her farewell. Turning to me, she leaned close to my ears and cupped her hands around my cheeks. She whispered, *"Pitit mouin,* little girl of mine, don't worry; it's all for the best, *TiFoune."* Her soft lips pressed a gentle kiss against my cheek; then she hugged me close to her chest with force. Her brown eyes were moist with emotion—a combination of hopefulness and helplessness.

"I will be okay, Mama," I said with naïve reassurance.

"I will see you again; don't you worry. Be good and listen to your father, but, more importantly, always be careful. Marie Renée Michaud, go and show the world what you are made of."

These were her last words.

My grandparents bid their goodbyes, and we all rushed through the airport gate in seconds. I turned back several times to take one last glimpse of my mother's beautiful face, not knowing if and when I would see her again.

Climbing the stairs to the airplane, in the open air I took a deep breath, held on to the rails with reluctant resolve, and turned around one last time, waving farewell to my beloved "Haiti *Cherie*." When I finally found my seat, I sat there motionless. I'd seen planes take off and land before, but I was about to experience what happens in between for the first time.

Suddenly, emerging feelings of anticipation for a better tomorrow and a better life consumed me. I was on my way. To where? I really didn't know.

Chapter 4
New Country, New Life, New Me

Embrace the New

I left Haiti, my soul-born country, at the age of thirteen. To say this was an ordinary circumstance would devalue its meaning. My life was on an intentional road toward promising opportunities, and I felt in my Haitian bones that an iron gate had opened, and my life would be changed forever.

One single plane ride was destined to alter my future. Getting on a plane to live in another country—not just any country, but the United States of America—was akin to winning the lottery, especially when coming from impoverished circumstances.

Excitement about seeing my father after being separated for four years, experiencing traveling on an aircraft for the first time, and knowing this could have been anyone's dream, but it was mine, was overwhelming. I sat quietly on the plane, watching other passengers, especially the elegantly dressed, neatly coiffed, and beautifully made-up flight attendants. Watching all the activities kept my brain from racing too much.

Not having seen him since I was nine, my father haunted my mind for many years, and now we would be reunited. *Who is he?* I pondered. *And what will living with him be like?*

Finally, bringing me back to the reality of the moment, the plane landed. Arriving at the airport in Miami and viewing its massive size threatened my security. The security of the familiar that I had left behind. I wasn't exposed to extravagances, so everything seemed novel and strangely overpowering.

We picked up our luggage and Uncle Jean's merchandise—mahogany carvings for his shop in New Hope—and swiftly cleared Immigration. As we walked through the airport, it was as if we were walking thorough an amusement park. I saw stores with fancy clothing, small shops displaying chocolate bars of every kind, and magazines and books overflowing on nearby shelves. I walked by restaurants and observed people of diverse shapes, sizes, and skin colors happily eating and drinking. Everyone was booming with energy. The air smelled different—cleaner, fresher, sporadic fumes of coffee. I secretly told myself, *I could learn to love this newfound country. Maybe as much as my homeland.* But then, *Don't be a traitor,* I thought to myself and smiled.

Finally, among the groups of overjoyed people who welcomed the newly arrived, there stood this distinguished, well-dressed man waving his arms in the air. I didn't recognize him at first, but as soon as my grandparents ran towards him and aggressively embraced him, I figured it out. It was my uncle Jean. I felt connected to Uncle Jean as soon as I recognized his glowing, deep-black skin and broad, flashy, playful smile.

"My dear *TiFoune*, little niece, you made it! Welcome to America!" he said in English, then quickly switched to Creole. "We worked so hard to get you here! Your papa's funny Serené name almost messed everything up." He chuckled.

I hadn't seen my uncle in a few years, and his greeting was so comforting; I felt immediately at home. But I covered my mouth to let out a soft giggle because I didn't completely understand when he spoke in English.

Then I started to think about where I actually was. I didn't know how America would welcome me, a young Black girl who doesn't know the country's spoken language. *Indeed, I will have no problem learning English. After all, I am told that I am very intelligent,* I thought. But then, inside, a critical dialogue started churning. I would find a way to use this to grow me, not bury me. I was ready for the challenge to fit in. New country, new life, new me.

Riding in my uncle Jean's minivan, which he fondly named the Blue Truck, we all set out for our destination, New Jersey. Looking out the car window, I felt empowered, unlike on my car ride when I left Haiti. The van was roomy, modern, and cool air burst out of the sides as soon as we climbed in. Until then, I had only been used to riding in the colorful *camionettes*[8] adorned with funny quotes that revealed the drivers' senses of humor. But, now, I was in America, the country that would certainly change my life for the better, and I was surrounded by family. My pounding heart was settling down.

We stopped at a popular fast-food restaurant for a meal. What was normal for Uncle Jean would prove to be bizarre for me. Rice and beans were an everyday staple in Haiti—that is, if one could afford them—so I asked for a portion of rice.

"May I have rice and beans, please? And do they have plantains?"

"*TiFoune*, my dear, this is an American fast-food restaurant. Those dishes aren't served here."

"Oh, really? How come? This is odd. What do people eat here?" I let escape out loud.

It's been a long day, and I am hungry for a plate of rice and beans with tassot.[9] *That's what I would like to have,* I thought to myself. But I quickly adjusted my manners. In Haiti, there is no verbal back-and-forth between adults and kids, so I remembered this and stayed quiet. The conversation ended there. Uncle Jean shook his head with amusement while I wondered, *Where is the rice-and-beans dish I'm used to eating?*

When a chunk of meat arrived with bread as its roof, and it was placed before me, I stared at this American meal with disgust. I lifted the top, a floppy bun, to discover onions, tomatoes, cheese, and lettuce, all mashed together with red sauce. *Is this pate tomate?*[10] I wondered to myself. No, I had just met my first cheeseburger. *Will this imposed way of life of eating fast food replace my delicious Haitian food?* I wondered. Regardless, I was too hungry to complain. I ate it all up. And, yes, I made sure I didn't make a mess on my brand-new pants suit. *Soon enough,* I reassured myself, *I will adjust and learn to love those burgers served with a little bag of* frites.[11]

My mind traveled back to those times when meat was very scarce, but rice and beans were plentiful. Haitians are very creative with their rice recipes. All varieties of beans and peas were a mainstay in the Haitian diet. Pinto beans, red kidney beans, black beans, lima beans, pigeon peas, sweet peas, and more beans and peas I couldn't name but loved. Of all the Haitian rice dishes imaginable, *diri ak djon,* the black-mushroom rice, made with a mushroom only found in Haiti, wins the gold medal. It is a symbol of our strength and our standing in the world as the magnificent Blacks. According to Haitians, women of Haiti make the best rice-and-beans dishes on the planet. It is further believed that a woman can only keep a husband if she knows how to prepare rice and beans to the proper Haitian standard.

We returned to the car and drove on what seemed to be the longest highway in the world. I was comforted that we were not squeezed into a tiny, crowded *tap tap*[12] driving on a dirt road overlooking cliffs with no rails. On this long ride to my father's house, caged between adults and their noisy Creole chatter, I thought again about life in Haiti. I reminisced about the humdrum days when my mother was in my life every day. Immediately, I started to miss her, and I felt as if I was going to cry. It hadn't even been twenty-four hours since I left! How was I ever going to survive this bitter separation? I struggled to maintain my composure and pretended to enjoy the conversations for the rest of the ride.

Finally, we all arrived at my father's place in New Jersey. The weather conditions changed gradually along the way. We went from a warm climate in Miami to a cold autumn day in New Jersey. So far, everything was much grander than I could have ever imagined. We approached the house; in my view, it was a palace. I marveled at the lime-green color. I loved it from my initial gaze and couldn't wait to go inside.

Uncle Jean opened the van door, allowing me to trail behind him, and then he wrapped a blanket around my shoulders. Everyone else climbed out of the van and stared at the house. Uncle Jean and I walked together toward the house and up to the stoop. He rang the buzzer.

Within seconds, the front door swung open, and there stood my father, wearing a serious face that eventually broke out into a broad smile. When I saw him for the first time, I stifled the excitement in my chest, but that didn't last long.

"Hey, Joe, I brought your precious daughter," said Uncle Jean.

"Thanks for bringing everyone in one piece, considering your driving history," my father responded sarcastically. This silliness, I would later learn, contributed to their affectionate, brotherly bond.

Still standing in the doorway, my father yelled out my name and some routine questions I didn't have time to answer.

"*TiFoune, TiFoune*, you made it, finally! Oh, my goodness, I am so happy. Did you enjoy the plane ride? Are you hungry?"

I didn't respond because I needed clarification on what he was saying, as he spoke half Creole and half English. Everything was happening so fast.

Then he turned to his parents and embraced them with hugs and kisses. "C'mon, everybody, welcome. Come in; come in; let's go up."

I was so amazed and got lost in my thoughts. *Joe? So now they call him Joe?*

My father continued to ask me question after question. I don't remember answering him. I could only see his dark-complexioned face flashing a cheery smile that seemed to widen before my eyes. We were together again. Others in the room were vaguely in the background while my world pirouetted faster and faster.

My father gave everyone a quick tour of the place, and when he showed us the bathroom, I thought there was no way that the latrine was inside the house. I would now be able to take a shower in private and not outside in public with a dress on. My father was pleased with my excitement when I saw that the kitchen was indoors, too. I ran into the living room and attempted to turn on the television. He watched me with a smile as I discovered all the luxuries of a real house.

My home was a castle, compared to where I used to live. While the adults talked in the living room about the journey, I sneaked into the other rooms. Could all this be mine to live in? My room was fully furnished with a six-drawer dresser, an oversized mirror, and two smaller tables next to a full-sized bed. And I had a closet! Small pink- and green-floral wallpaper surrounded me. I had never seen anything like it.

Suddenly, I felt a pang of loneliness. I would have to get accustomed to sleeping in a room all by myself. Until that day, I had slept in a one-room home with my mother, my brother, my nieces, and the other lady who helped us with housework. Lost in my thoughts, I suddenly heard my father's voice.

"Open up your valises, take the hangers out of the closet, and hang your clothes. Then put the small items in the *chiffonier*."

I followed his orders immediately and started unpacking my few belongings. Excitement was my only emotion, aside from mild shock. This lifestyle didn't match my expectations; it surpassed them.

"Come. Let's go outside. I have something else to show you." Once outside, my father pointed to a car, a Mercury Grand Marquis. "You did say that your favorite color was blue, right?"

I giggled because I knew I couldn't drive, but my father was beaming with joy.

"Nothing is too good for my future doctor."

I had learned at an early age that my father expected me to become a medical doctor; from a very tender age, I remember that he repeated his views often. This was his vision for his only daughter, so he cleverly sent for me right before I entered the most important academic years of my life at thirteen. I was a part of his life's mission.

My uncle and everyone I'd traveled with since I landed in the new country left shortly thereafter. After the excitement began to wear off, my father and I relaxed in the kitchen, sitting across from each other and discussing plans for the week. I had something on my mind that I needed to voice. The conflict within me about not having my mother join me was soon a reality I could no longer ignore, and I needed answers from my father.

"When will Mama come?"

His response was abrupt. "I will send for your mother as soon as I can." Then he leaned toward me and squeezed my cheek. "Your education is the priority right now for you!"

"Sure, Papa." I accepted his response. After all, he was my father. The one who had worked diligently for years to secure an educational opportunity for me.

Still, all I wanted was my mother's loving embrace at that moment.

Chapter 5
Life with Papa
Discovery and Adaptation

Within a few days of arriving, I was told Thanksgiving in America was approaching. A celebration at my father's house was planned, which included my arrival as the main event. I was my father's daughter, and he wanted to broadcast my arrival to everyone.

Haitian friends and family gathered on Thanksgiving Day to meet Joe's only daughter, *TiFoune*, the apple of his eye. I had an awakening in my mind that day; it felt as if I was being offered a new life, and it was based solely on my arrival in America. The guests brought Haitian food of all kinds. It seemed an eternity since I'd had real Haitian food. White rice, red-kidney-beans sauce, fried plantains, and French-cut green beans—all made it feel like home, the home that now seemed a lifetime ago.

I ate my first Thanksgiving roasted turkey, which I had never seen cooked whole in my entire life. In a way, it was an initiation into the traditional American culture. *Everything will prove to be for the better,* I thought. But on that celebratory day, I learned more about my father's human struggles and how they would affect my own life going forward.

After experiencing my first American holiday, clothes shopping was soon on the agenda. The clothes I wore to take those stressful three-day certificate exams in Haiti were my entire wardrobe: three vibrantly colored summer dresses and a delicate beige-polyester bell-bottom pants suit that I wore on travel day. A wintry season was nearing, so I needed clothes suited for cold weather. This change of seasons was fascinating. The world I now belonged to had something better in store for me—a stylish American wardrobe to go with the changing seasons. I soon learned that living in the Northeast meant that I could dress for four distinct seasons—fall, winter, spring, and summer.

Altering wardrobes for different seasons added a new dimension to my life. It was almost as if I were changing personalities each season; the choices were to follow a trend, create your own, or wear the same thing year after year. Style had never been introduced into my world before, so this variation appealed to me.

But I never expected to go on a shopping excursion with my father as part of the introduction into American fashionwear. Shopping with a father who knew nothing about teenage-girls' clothing was an awkward experience. That's all I can say. But I needed an overhaul, and soon.

"Papa, are we going to buy more clothes for me?"

"Why? Didn't you bring enough clothes? Your dresses should last you through the winter."

I smiled, but I wasn't sure if he was being funny or not, as I had only brought summer dresses with me. "Papa, it's brutally cold outside, and my clothes aren't warm enough."

"Sure, young lady, let's plan a day to shop!"

I began to think he had no clue about buying girl clothes, and I picked up on his uneasiness. He was my father, not my mother.

Mama would instantly know my needs, but now that I had a dad in charge, things would be different. Mama used to buy the fabrics, then take me to the local seamstress who would take my measurements, and, afterward, we would peruse catalogues until we spotted dresses that were appealing to me. A few days later, I would return for the first fitting, and my dresses were ready within a week.

Now, my role was morphing into guiding my father so that he could, in turn, guide me. He caught on and scheduled a trip to take me clothes shopping. I then realized that life with Papa would be interestingly different.

When the weekend came, my father took me to Downtown Trenton, where the trendy shops were. We strolled around a bit before I chose a random women's clothing boutique. Still not used to the chilly weather, I shivered as I opened the store's door. I wanted to be inside more than anything. Walking around and feeling so cold didn't make sense to me. I came from Haiti's hot and steamy island; however, having to get used to the cold was my new reality.

It was a bit awkward going on outings with my father, but I told myself that I would get accustomed to it. Not that I didn't want to be with him, I just missed being with my mother more than anything. Getting used to having only a father didn't set in overnight.

As we entered the boutique, I anticipated my father's cluelessness.

"Hello, may I help you?" offered a well-dressed saleswoman; she spoke directly to my father.

"We are looking for clothes to fit this young lady."

"Certainly! What is her current size?"

"I think I'm a small," I whispered in Creole to my father, who was serving as a translator.

He told the saleslady my size in English.

"Right this way."

We passed the undergarments section, and he said to the saleswoman, "She needs those, too," pointing to the rack.

My head instantly dropped. I looked down at the floor as we all walked toward the middle of the store. I was embarrassed for myself and for him. It wasn't as if I was consumed with shame, but I instinctively realized that shopping with my father seemed weird; it really ought to be my mother. It was a mild mismatch. But, inside, I knew that my new life was different, and I needed to accept that.

I left that afternoon with a plush, tan-colored coat, a woolen hat, a scarf and gloves, pants, multicolored knitted socks, undergarments, and a few bulky sweaters. Dressing for the threatening cold felt adventurous, and I was ready. Snow boots were a necessity, too, so I bought my first pair. I couldn't wait to go home to my room and model the first clothes I had just bought in America.

Undoubtedly, I was astonished at how many clothes I could buy at the same time. Money was no object to my father. In fact, he was encouraging me to get all that I needed. I felt as if I were one of those rich girls at *École Mere Louise, my elementary school in Haiti.* The shopping mission was a success.

Chapter 6
Assimilation, Separation, and Determination

As if nothing else was odd in my life, starting school was the next step that created its own set of difficulties. The middle school had both girls and boys. I was accustomed to an all-girls school. Then after each class period, all the students left the classroom to go to the next. But to top it all off, I did not understand a word of English. However, to my advantage, I was paired with the school's French teacher who served as my translator and helped me navigate the school day.

While I was learning to speak English, my classmates were aggressively studying and involved in various school activities and fostering friendships. I was beginning to suspect that my father's expectations of my mastering this new language sooner than later would be a challenging feat.

The rules were set. "English will be the *only* spoken language in our home," my father informed me firmly. Adopting another language using his method created fear and embarrassment for me when I spoke and mispronounced words.

While adjusting to the American culture was the primary concern for me at the time, I was also dealing with homesickness and missing my mother, my siblings, and my friends in Haiti. Knowing that my situation was not about to change, I had to learn to embrace my new life, as progress often comes at a cost. Separation, assimilation, and determination would be my ongoing life themes.

If clothes shopping with my father was embarrassing, living with him through puberty was an even more uncomfortable strain. Puberty was hard enough to go through, in and of itself, let alone without my mother. When my menses began, I was secretive so my father wouldn't find out. I decided not to allow him to join me on this part of my growing journey since he was a man and clueless about being a young girl; at least, that's what I thought.

But one day, I slipped up and forgot to flush the evidence. When he confronted me, it was an awkward confession of some kind on his part. It was obvious that he wasn't too comfortable with this adolescent milestone. He mumbled something to the effect of "I *see you have a monthly now.*" As I stood there, angry with myself for allowing my secret to be discovered, he continued speaking, hardly looking at me, "I asked the neighbor next door to assist you. She will drive you to the local pharmacy."

I returned home, feeling shameful, and found it difficult to talk or look him in the eye, so I raced straight to my room. I hated my life and wanted back my old life with my mother. From then on, I discerned my father could never substitute for my mother. And I should learn what I needed on my own.

Life moved on, and we learned to occupy the same space as father and daughter. In time, he would share other necessary life skills with me, which added to my development as a young girl. Strange as it seems, my father taught me how to function in the kitchen; his cooking and cleaning skills were methodical, and I loved following his directions.

At times, I cast my eyes on him and giggled because, in Haiti, it was unconventional for a man to prepare meals, let alone wear an apron. Sometimes we concocted recipes together. It didn't matter whether it was flavorless or flawless; we ate what we created.

During the preparation of the meal, we'd clean the kitchen with such rigor, as if we were in the military, and it had to pass inspection. *"Clean as you go; wipe each splash as it happens. Don't let it dry up. The kitchen must look as if you were never in there when the cooking is done. You must always remember that. You hear me, young lady?"* To this day, my kitchen sparkles, regardless of how much cooking I've done. I thank him for this life-skill habit.

Despite all of the uncomfortable adolescent years, I marched on. My English skills improved, and I was beginning to assimilate into my environment successfully. Education was a force in my life that kept me dreaming and wanting more for my family back in Haiti…and for me. When my high school years arrived, my father enrolled me in a private Catholic school. I had attended one week in public school, but after he witnessed a pregnant student walking out of the building when he picked me up, I was abruptly transferred. He didn't want me in a place where teenage girls could attend school while pregnant. "This is not a healthy moral environment for my future doctor," he said.

Attending the Catholic school placed me in an environment with about two hundred students. This smaller setting was beneficial for me. I could navigate the building easily, and I received the specialized attention I desperately needed in all subject areas, especially in mathematics. Math was problematic for me; my brain was wired for the metric system, so the adjustment was difficult. On the other hand, the uniform requirement was familiar to me because this was the norm in Haiti. Assimilating into a culture and country that held a promising future didn't come without confusion and struggle.

My father had a few paranoid idiosyncrasies that I didn't understand, but to which I adjusted. One year, my ninth-grade French class spent months learning the play *Louise*, and then the school planned a trip to New York City to see the original Broadway performance. My father refused to let me attend—*"No, and that's that"*—with no explanation. He wasn't secure about my traveling to the city.

I wanted desperately to belong in all ways; assimilation had many endless levels, and I found myself moving from one adjustment to the next. Ultimately, I learned to accept disappointments and leverage challenges as opportunities. This helped to build my resilient internal framework.

Time passed with fewer dilemmas, and months turned into years. I worked diligently on my academics, staying on track so that someday I could become a doctor and make my father proud. Many immigrants had lifelong dreams about earning an education in America, and my father handed this opportunity to me, his only daughter. Where I came from, without the financial means, finishing primary school was unprecedented, and entering a university was certainly a monumental feat. Shifting a family lineage into another social class meant an elevation of power for future generations. I was determined to secure this for my family.

While growing up in America, my thoughts wandered back to Haiti. Sadly, there, poverty was a dominating factor in my family climate. In our boxlike house, which was technically an oversized room, we studied by gas lamps to get assignments done for school, while others cooked or cleaned around the crowdedness to earn their keep. Our surroundings were constantly in motion. It was a community effort of sorts, a cluster of survivors.

When my mother was nine years old, she was displaced and joined another family because her mother appeared to have abandoned her. In her twenties, they reunited, and she learned about the circumstances behind the situation. It is common for Haitians to travel to other islands in the Caribbean when they have financial difficulties, or to move to America or Europe. My maternal grandparents moved to Cuba, where my mother and her siblings were born. After a few years, my maternal grandparents, whom I never met, took my mother back to Haiti to a boarding school. Because of an unfortunate diplomatic event between Haiti and Cuba, my mother was separated from her family.

Poverty and helplessness in third-world countries can result in devastating transitions, driving people to make desperate decisions, even regarding their children. My mother never shared her story of separation from her parents with us until I was an adult, but, had she told me, I wonder if I would have shown more resistance to leaving her behind.

Missing my mother continued to etch a scar in my teenage heart. I wanted and needed to share my life with her. Whenever I approached my father about when he would send for her, he brushed me off without reason or explanation. This intensified the hurt. Trying to reach my father's heart proved pointless.

We repeated the familiar discussion over the course of a few years, the subject always the same—when would my mother join us? But the conversation seemed to go in a circular motion, never reaching any resolution.

It started at school. I overheard some classmates talking about how their family was planning a surprise celebration for their mother. In America, Mother's Day is at the beginning of May, and in Haiti, there's a designated Haitian Mother's Day, which is the last Sunday of May. With all of these celebrations, Mama was on my mind more than ever. Desperately, I needed my father to finally, once and for all, bring Mama to America!

During dinner one evening, sitting across the table from my father, I put my fork down, looked directly into his eyes, and spoke in a low voice, "Papa, are you going to send for Mama soon?"

"What? Now is not a good time to discuss that subject."

"Well, I've been here for almost two years, and I thought I would see her by now, especially after I got settled in school."

"I don't want to talk about this. I already told you it will be as soon as I can!"

"Mama wrote to me and said you would probably send for her soon. Did you speak with her about this?"

"Quit bugging me! Just eat your dinner. You are beginning to sound like a broken record."

"Papa," I said, lowering my voice even more as I enunciated each word, "what is the plan?"

At this point, his patience had worn out; he looked me straight in the eyes and said some words that I never thought I would hear. "As a matter of fact," he said in a calm but determined voice, "I'm not sending for her, and that's my final word!" The frightening glare in his eyes revealed the truth—he never planned to send for Mama. "I want you to become an educated American. This is my only concern. You don't need your mother to do it. So be quiet!"

His words pierced through me emotionally as if I were being physically stabbed. My eyes welled up with pools of tears, and my heart pounded with painful throbs. I was consumed by hurt and confusion. Hatred was steaming in my Haitian bones; I hated my father at that very moment. Still, the betrayal I was facing made me question his motives. Was he really that cruel? Separating a mother from her only daughter showed another side of his character. *Who is this man with whom I am living? What does he want from me?* I began to wonder. *Is it possible he stole me from my mother?*

Changing the tone of my voice, I tried to appeal to his human side. I was relentless. "Why won't you help her, Papa?"

"If you want your mother to come here, you'll have to figure it out yourself. Enough about this. I'm going to sleep." He got up and left the table. He stomped into his room and slammed the door so hard that the noise slapped reality into me. I had heard him loud and clear. Finally, an answer. My father's mind was set. His intentions were only to help me, and my mother's life was of no concern to him.

The thought of never seeing Mama again was inconceivable. *How do I find my way back home?* Running out of the house crossed my mind. But where would I go? Who would help me? I think they were all in on it. I went to my room, sobbing and feeling defeated, scared, and resentful.

Thereafter, whenever I brought up this subject, my father hurried off and avoided a resolution altogether. But my obstinate teenage mind wanted answers to soothe my aching feelings of homesickness for my mother. Holding in these divided loyalties choked me emotionally. My father—the one to whom I was deeply grateful for accelerating my life into the fast lane—had exiled my mother from my life. Even as a growing teen, I knew his actions were a form of alienation.

Before coming to America, I never thought to ask my father if and when he would send for my mother. I just assumed that as a parent, he would want his only daughter to have a mother in her life. Missing my mother, on top of everything to which I had to adjust, created a wedge between my father and me.

I endured profound helplessness. Immigration papers and traveling documents were something I knew nothing about. I felt left in a lurch and abandoned by my father. I obsessed over the situation, asking myself constantly, *How am I going to make it happen? I am only fifteen years old! Who can I share this with? Certainly not Mama.*

Well, I finally thought to myself, *if I can't change his mind, I have to devise a plan to make him support Mama and the family back home.*

It worked; my warning that I will quit school and find employment forced him into action. He continued to supply me with money to send back home to Haiti. At times, I had to trick him into giving me the money, but I had to make sure Mama's rent was paid. My mother cared for my brother Max's two children, her grandchildren, so when they needed uniforms, textbooks, and supplies to continue with their schooling, help was on the way. In this way, my father was responsible for my mother's well-being and that of others, so this soothed my disappointment in him.

Even though, in the end, my father didn't let us down financially, I just didn't want to keep living with him. His chronic illnesses had left him with anxieties that he could not control. As time passed, I realized that he was who he was, and there was no changing him. I had to get used to this life. Mothering a father wasn't the ideal life for a young teenage girl, but I was hopeful things would change.

Did I come to America to trade my sanity in exchange for a successful future? My rebounding mindset kept me on a steady track. I would and could turn it around. I stayed focused on my schooling and kept in contact with my mother. And I vowed to myself that I would send for her someday. I promised this to my heart.

Not only did I send money back home, but also I was able to send parcels through family acquaintances when they traveled back to Haiti. They all felt sorry for me and my helpless situation. They saw me as a modern-day, young *Cosette* living with an old man, as in Victor Hugo's classic book *Les Misérables*. Clothes and a few luxuries were always on their way to my mother. Since my father didn't limit how much I could buy, I sent as much as possible.

Once, I even convinced a family member traveling to Haiti to take a small television set to my mother on my behalf. It wasn't the biggest, but it was a grand prize for someone in Haiti. Later on in life, I attended a funeral in Philadelphia where I met a woman from Haiti who knew my mother when she had the TV in her home. She shared a fond recollection of how my mother would offer TV-watching and movie-time events and welcome all the neighbors to her porch. This woman's eyes glowed with appreciation as she told me about those happy times of being able to witness another world with her own eyes by watching TV. She said the Haitian community lived vicariously through the shows, between American sitcoms and soap operas. This made their days more enjoyable, and they even learned some English. I left that conversation with a sense of pure inner purpose, knowing that I contributed somehow to the happiness of people beyond my immediate family in Haiti, my homeland.

In return, my mother sent me simple gifts that she could afford—small jars of fresh organic peanut butter, which spoiled me, as I found it hard to settle for the peanut butter in American supermarkets; embroidered handkerchiefs; *dous makos*, a layered, vanilla-strawberry-and-chocolate fudge; and dry herbal-tea leaves.

Her lengthy letters included family updates and were always full of motherly advice.

Mama's efforts to keep the mother-daughter bond in place were apparent. She longed for our relationship to stay alive and connected until we were reunited again. Deep down, I think she knew there was a chance she might never see me again. All the while, I hoped and prayed that one day I would be able to see her beautiful face before my full, fleshy, youthful cheeks shed completely as my teenage years were disappearing.

Chapter 7
Papa's Changing Mind
Never Give Up

Summer was in the air, and the end of another school year was slowly approaching. I was stressing over end-of-year tests and begging my father to let me volunteer at the local hospital. I was also thinking about the school break ahead of me. With all that was happening, I missed Mama terribly, too.

Short conversations on the phone with her were tearful and frustrating. Some days it wasn't easy to get a grip on my feelings. Life dealt me this experience for which no one had prepared me—how to function in life without my mother and handle my father's ways. Even though he worked hard to take care of me and provide for the family back home, his refusal to even speak with Mama was taking its toll on me.

In each letter from my mother, she tried to convince me that living with Papa was a sacrifice that had to be made for the sake of the entire family. After all, I was in America, living out an immigrant's dream. *Or is it a nightmare?* Our phone conversations replayed the same dialogue without a resolution.

"Hello, Mama! Is everything good with you?"

"*TiFoune, TiFoune.* Don't you worry about your mama. I'm doing very well. Please be a good student, and in time I'll see your pretty face again," she said, trying to calm my emotions.

"I know…I know, but I want to be with you. Haiti is my home, and I miss everything!"

"It's going to happen, so give it more time. Remember what you are there for. Focus on the goal. America will give you a chance to become anything you want to be in life. Be patient. Rome wasn't built in one day. Be patient!"

"But sometimes it's difficult for me. I have a lot of studying, and I'm still working on my English. And, Mama, there aren't many Haitians in my school, so I feel alone and different."

"Good, stay different. Uniqueness has its advantages. Capitalize on what makes you different."

My complaints continued, "And sometimes Joe—I mean Papa—acts loud, mean, and stupid."

My attempt to tell on him didn't cause my mother to withdraw with worry. She knew of his ways but counted on my maturity to make light of it. So hearing about his behavior didn't make her flinch. She realized that I was making a sacrifice, an ultimate sacrifice.

"Be strong, *TiFoune*, my little girl. Nothing lasts forever. This too will someday pass."

I felt her motherly support through the long-distance telephone lines; her words, wrapped in wisdom, gave me inner strength. She knew what to say and how to say it, and after speaking with her, nothing could stop me from designing my future. And she was right. Despite three years of complaining about my father and wanting her to come to America, nothing was forever.

One evening, I decided to stand up to my father again. Arriving from work, he always grabbed the daily mail from the kitchen counter, then headed over to his weathered, brown-leather recliner, put his feet up, and proceeded to rip open and read the mail. I knew it was a perfect time to speak with him.

This time I will get through to him, I thought. *He will listen to my pleas and know how much it means to me to see my own mother.*

I sat down at the end of the sofa, close to the recliner in which he was going through his daily ritual, and took a meaningful breath. Affixing my eyes on him, I began my speech, which I had practiced in my head for the past week. Casually, I began a conversation with my father as if I were an old friend, "Hey, Joe!"

"Yo."

"Can we talk for a minute?"

"What is it now? You want to buy your mom a new Frigidaire on my credit card, like you did when you bought the TV?"

His responses often distracted my focused thinking, but this time I acted a bit more combative, instead of like a scared cat. I wanted answers, and I wanted them right there and then. What better time to do it than while he was still in a good mood. "Nope, it's too heavy anyway," I said jokingly. "There is no amount of begging that I can do that would make someone take one to Haiti for me. But it won't stop me from trying though."

When I got no response, I continued, "Seriously, can you please listen to me?"

Still opening the mail and reading one particular letter, he stopped in suspended animation, looked at me, and said flatly, "What?"

I wasn't ready to say anything. I froze. Then I took another deep breath and let my words travel from my mouth to his ears, "It's been way too long since I've seen Mama. I want her here! I mean it." I felt a whimper coming on, but I held on to my emotions.

Silence.

He turned his eyes to the mail he was opening, then dropped an envelope on his lap, and stared straight ahead. Without looking at me, he began to speak, "I told you before, and I'll tell you again; I'm not sending for your mother.

Stability | The Belle of the Ball

There is no point. When you can make it happen, you can do it when you get much older. Right now, no is my answer."

Silence.

I didn't know what to say. Like a good daughter, I followed his lead and sat in silence. I had endured three years without my mother. I had intentionally focused on school and set it as a priority, while simultaneously assimilating into the American culture. *Why is it so difficult for him to empathize and understand what I need?* I asked myself.

I began to think that getting on that plane to the United States was a massive mistake, not that I had any choice in the decision process. Coming to America to prove that I could earn an education and become a doctor to please my father—now, that seemed as if it was someone else's dream at my expense. Nothing made me happy anymore, and I wasn't sure that I could continue with life the way it was.

Then my father turned his head towards me. I was still sitting there, staring down at the floor, and wondering what to say next that would change his mind.

"Okay, *TiFoune*. I will make a plan."

"Really?!"

"Yes. But the plan will be for you to visit your mother. That would be best. So you don't have to worry about getting any documentation for her. It will be simpler if you go and visit."

He had turned a corner and listened to me. I was more elated than he would ever know. I thought about what he had just said. My eyes started to move from side to side as if my brain were calculating if it all made sense. This meant that I would see Haiti again. I would visit the land, the people, my brother, my nieces, my friends, and, most importantly, my dear mother.

Then…it all registered. Burning with enthusiasm, I leaped from the couch, threw my arms around my father's neck, and hugged him with all of the stored hope that had grown inside of me over the past three drawn-out years. That was one of the very few times I showed affection toward him. I could breathe easier. My father's change of mind invited happiness into my world. I learned that day that perseverance is the key to all closed doors.

The plan was to visit Mama during the summer break of my sixteenth year. I had a joyous skip in my step at the end of the school year, knowing that I would soon see her. I left Haiti as a thirteen-year-old girl off to the wondrous land of the Americas to live out the dream of becoming a doctor and changing the family legacy. Now, I was returning as a promising, prospective college student.

The journey hadn't been easy; there were unexpected joys and uninvited challenges, but I was stronger for all the experiences. The following week, the arrangements were made, and I was set to leave when school ended. Everything was falling into place.

Chapter 8
Hope Still Springs

The joy slightly diminished when Joe announced he would join me on my trip to Haiti. I wasn't expecting that. We were dropped off at the airport by one of his friends. This was my first time driving past the Statue of Liberty, and seeing it made me think about the freedom for a better life that it supposedly promised. In my mind, I was secretly planning to fight for my freedom when I got to Haiti. I would never ever set foot back in America again.

It was my second time on a plane. We boarded the flight. I sat quietly and contemplated my getaway plan.

Hours later, we arrived! Sweltering heat engulfed my body as we left the airport and entered the streets of Haiti. America's summer days were hot and humid, but feeling Haiti's tropical heat reminded me of its unforgiving heat waves. Immediately, I missed my air-conditioned, privileged American home.

A friend of my father greeted us at the airport and drove us to my mother's home. On the way, I began noticing things to which I hadn't paid much attention before. Some homes were brightly painted like works of art. Tired-looking donkeys on dirt roads passed by. Merchants were selling fruits and vegetables on either side of the main road. Stray dogs were sniffing around for any substance or edible morsel of food, and women were carrying heavy loads of merchandise on their heads. Goats were eating out of the garbage scattered on the ground as *tap-tap camio-nettes* took school children home.

Disturbing as it all was, I was back in Haiti, and I wanted to be there; I needed to be there. I was home.

My mother had no information about my arrival. I suspect my father wanted to surprise her. However, the plans were somewhat last-minute, and he didn't contact her by telephone to let her know we were coming. When we reached her house on Center Street, she wasn't there. So we decided to wait by her unit.

Neighbors were shocked to see me. "*TiFoune* is here; *TiFoune* is here. I can't believe it. I can't believe it. She's back."

Everything seemed so surreal. Within the blink of an eye, everybody in the *lakou dis pieces* was in front of my mother's unit. All my friends were hugging and kissing me, and I couldn't help but notice they looked so different. I had changed, too. They were amazed at my weight gain and offered me many compliments. In Haiti, being malnourished was common. If you were overly thin, it could reveal how poor your family was.

While reacquainting myself with friends, someone rushed to find my mother to tell her that her daughter was home. It was Saturday, and she was praying at the time in the *Eglise de Dieu de la Rue du Centre,* the Church of God of Center Street. That was her routine, a fasting prayer from morning to noon to pray for those she loved. In the meantime, my emotions were erupting and escalating simultaneously. I wasn't sure if I would bawl my eyes out or chant with cheer. All I remember was a stream of pent-up feelings. Finally, I was home, and I had a plan.

While I waited for my mother's return, I scanned the area, and for the first time, I recognized the stretch of poverty all around. The clothes that the natives wore were simple and worn. Kids were playing outside with no shoes; there were small boys wearing only a shirt with no pants. Ladies were preparing meals outside using *chaudières*[13] on coal *fourneaux.*[14] Life was untangling before my eyes in a way for which I had no words. Suddenly, I felt privileged. Living the past three years in America would be considered a life of luxury to most Haitians.

But I was still the same person inside.

Mama came running down the road with a smile broader than my own. When I realized it was she, I started running toward her. She grabbed me aggressively as I went to kiss her cheek; then I kissed her again and again. My mother hugged me so tight that I felt her heart pulsating against me. I was like a rag doll in her arms, powerless and limp.

Overwhelmed, she spoke loudly, *"TiFoune, TiFoune,* little girl of mine, *pitit mouin.* Here in Haiti! Unbelievable! I'm so, so happy."

"Mama, I'm so, so happy to be here, too!"

Looking up toward the sky, with her arms raised in the air, she continued, "God, you are good! What a miracle! My daughter is right here with me! Praise be the Lord! Oh, and your dad fed you well, I see. Why didn't you write to me and let me know, so I could prepare for your arrival?"

"Oh, I guess Papa didn't tell you." I gave him a mean look. I didn't understand his feelings for my mother anymore, and I wasn't sure how they would behave with each other.

We continued chatting about simple things, and I noticed my father was quietly waiting on the side. There was no surprise the reunion between my mother and father didn't happen as I had hoped. After seven years since his departure from our house, my father stayed long enough to greet my mother before his friend urged him to leave with him.

"C'mon, Joe; let's go. We need to go home," his friend said with authority.

I was okay with my father going to stay somewhere else. My reunion belonged only to us now—mother and daughter. I just wanted to be home with her.

After she calmed down, I explained how my father had finally turned a corner, changed his mindset, and planned the trip. *"It all happened so fast, Mama. I kept insisting, and finally he broke down."*

I don't believe she cared about how it happened. All that mattered was that I was near her, and she could see me with her own two eyes. Others around watched us as we joyously chatted a bit. Then my mother grabbed my hand to take me inside her unit. Some neighbors were still giddy and chatting in Creole about how I looked. I tried to answer some of their random questions, but my mother's insistent pulling and talking dominated the scene. Her daughter was home, and she wanted all of my attention.

The size of my mother's place looked much smaller than before. The one big room I left three years ago still had only the bare necessities for living: mattresses, makeshift closets, crates for storage, a table, chairs, and the wooden family stool. It was comfortable at the beginning of my stay, but I was used to my own room, indoor plumbing, and a full kitchen with a gas stove and refrigerator. Still, I loved being around my mother, visiting friends, eating authentic Haitian food, and living a humble life. No pressure at all. Life was simple again.

The novelty of my return wore off the first week. I remember this because I started helping my mother with the daily cooking and cleaning. But to my surprise, I welcomed doing anything, including the arduous chores.

While separating beans from random pebbles, I consciously revisited the decision in my head to remain in Haiti. When I lived in America, my world consisted of a litany of competitive aspirations, primarily educational. The thrill of academic achievements lost its luster in the mix of my father's overindulgences and the constant pressure of my trying to acquiesce to the culture. The lifestyle in Haiti demanded less of me. Most worries were financial, which now seemed manageable. Funds were coming in from my father; after completing school, I could work, get a decent-paying job, and contribute. Thoughts about staying in Haiti circulated in my head, so I shared them with my mother.

"Mama, I missed being home—here in Haiti, that is. All the neighbors, your food, your smile, my big brother, and my little nieces."

"Of course, of course, you miss it. This is your first home."

"Yeah, well, I think I will stay right here. I can go back to America when I'm much older."

"*TiFoune*, do you mean to stay here? And not go back to America?" Her face contorted a bit, and she froze while she waited for my response.

"Yes, here. I love being back home! Did you see I took a bucket and went to fetch water with the neighborhood kids yesterday? I am re-assimilating just fine. After all, I was only gone for three years."

My mother stood silently. I was still working on cleaning out the beans, and she was quietly ironing some clothes in the corner. I had expected jubilation. I had expected a squeal of glee. I had expected kisses and hugs. I hadn't expected silence.

She turned her head towards me. Putting the iron down, she walked closer to where I was. I suddenly felt a knot in my stomach and a rumbling in my gut.

"You cannot come back here to stay, *TiFoune*. The life here is not for you. You have to figure out a way to embrace your *new* life."

I rechecked her words in my head. "Yes, but what if I want to stay? Are you saying you wouldn't want me here?"

"I want you here, my little girl, but what I want…and what must happen…are two different things."

No one in this world is on my side, I thought. They only want misery for me. Nobody understands my dilemma. I felt so alone.

"Why do you wish for me to go back there? Do you know what I have to deal with? Father is a good man, but he struggles with insecurities and paranoia. Once, I was playing in the backyard, and for some reason, he started to chase me with a pole. Another time, he threw a carved wooden statue at me because I didn't do well in math. It landed on my head. I was bleeding, Mama."

She didn't say a word. Her head was tilted down toward the floor; I saw nothing that resembled any form of emotion.

Mentioning my father's physical disciplinary ways to my mother left the air as soon as my words ended. Parents lashing out at their children wasn't questioned in Haiti. I did notice a flicker of concern in my mother's eyes when she finally looked up, but sympathy couldn't outweigh what was at stake—*a promising future for all*. Besides, children were roughed up in Haiti all the time, and that wouldn't change because of me.

When my mother spoke, her response rendered a stance of clarity and finality for me. "*TiFoune*, I have an idea of what you are going through."

"If you do, then let me stay." My heart hurt. Going back to America, living with Papa, missing Mama, day in and day out, and learning the local lifestyle in all ways was so stressful for me. I wasn't sure it was all worth it. "Mama, please, please. I want to be here in Haiti. I don't think you understand! In America, if a parent hurts a child, they could get in serious trouble and go to jail. I had to go to the hospital and get stitches. I had to lie about how I got hurt."

"*Pitit mouin*, she choked out, her eyes filled with pleading, "what fate awaits us and the next generation if you choose to stay in Haiti? What will become of us?" she whispers.

It was at that moment I realized my reality. I had lost the battle. I couldn't stay with Mama, the one I had prayed for and had longed to be with for years. *But is she betraying me? I wondered.* My words meant nothing. She wasn't listening to my pleas. My mother's silence penetrated my thoughts.

Stability | The Belle of the Ball

"You can't stay. *TiFoune*, your father is helping us because you are there in America to make it happen. And you need to continue your education to become a success, make money, and help this family to survive. I am counting on you. The family is counting on you. Future generations are counting on you," she said with a tone of seriousness I'd never heard before.

So there it was. The decision to stay in Haiti was not in my hands.

I eventually convinced myself that I had to return to America. The next few days, I attempted to enjoy time with friends and Mama, even though I dreaded returning to America.

When the day arrived, I boarded the plane with the heaviness of defeat in my soul. *No use looking back, I thought. She doesn't care if she never sees me again.* With tears pouring down, I took my seat knowing that a part of me had died. Somehow, I knew that my childhood was behind me.

My mother needed my father, and she probably always would. This was the culture; women relied on men, no matter the sacrifice. Women in Haiti lived without a voice or an opportunity for a future. I had the responsibility to cross the line of poverty that I inherited. My parents were paving the way for me. They gave me life and mental strength, and my duty was to outperform my familial roots.

Although I had hoped my mother would relinquish her role as my guiding force and let me stay in Haiti, she taught me differently. I learned that becoming who I was meant to be would take more than courage; it demanded sacrifice. I was my mother's lifeline, and she was looking out for everyone's greater good. I knew exactly what she was doing, but it hurt.

"What will become of us?" My mother's words echoed in my head.

What *would* become of her and those for whom she cared? They would do without if I didn't go back and work toward my future financial goals. I couldn't bear the thought.

So that was that. Any idea of my staying in Haiti was removed from my consciousness. After everything I had experienced over the past several years, all I could think was, *Hope still springs within me.*

Still, every day, my longing for a mother in my life visited my mind during those tender teenage years.

Chapter 9
The Ultimate Pursuit

My high school years presented me with second thoughts about whether or not I would academically qualify to enter medical school. Mastering the English language, learning a new math system, and assimilating into the American culture became my life's struggles. And fitting in was a constant personal dilemma, not to mention my father's dream of my becoming a doctor. This was his purpose for luring me to America—to attain a college education in medicine and fulfill his dream, the ultimate pursuit.

Besides reveling in the moment of seeing Mama, my brother, my nieces, my friends, and everything I hold dear, my family in Haiti experienced a major victory. My oldest brother, Max, and his wife, who under the Duvalier regime had been detained in a political prison, were suddenly released. This was the result of President Carter's administration demanding the release of all political prisoners in Haiti. Fearing for their lives, my brother, his wife, and my two nieces left Haiti permanently for France.

Mama was happy that her son and his wife had survived the ordeal. But separating abruptly from her granddaughters, whom she had been taking care of for the past six years, was more than she could bear. Coincidentally, a family member, whose girlfriend had a two-year-old infant girl they couldn't take care of, showed up at Mama's door.

"Auntie Aline, we need your help," the young mother frantically spoke.

"How can I help you, my girl?"

"We have tried, but we can't properly take care of the baby." Without stopping, she continued to disclose how the past two years had been difficult for her and the baby. "We can no longer stay at the room we rented. I am begging you to please take my baby and raise her. You are the only one I trust."

Such situations, though not ideal, often occur to parents dealing with inadequate circumstances. In any case, Mama agreed to raise the girl as her own without any official document.

With everyone seemingly happy all around the world, life returned to normalcy. But, not long after, the family in America suffered a colossal loss; Uncle Jean was in pain and went to Princeton Hospital for a routine surgical procedure. To this day, we don't know what went wrong, but our beloved Uncle Jean unexpectedly took a turn for the worse and died. No one on my father's side of the family was ever the same again. We were all in shock. My grandmother was inconsolable. My grandfather adopted a perpetually stoic demeanor, and we could no longer read his emotions. His young wife was devastated. Joe and his siblings led the mourning procession. Our beloved Jean, the family's patriarch, left Earth at the young age of forty without much warning. He drove himself to the hospital and never returned. We felt the void for years to come.

Uncle Jean left his wife, Jeannette, with two young infants. Nurturing Papa's bad ways and my desperate emotional need to have my mother with me was so overwhelming that I began latching on to my aunt Jeannette. We were both suffering, but Aunt Jeannette was resilient. With my uncle in his celestial rest, I visited her on the weekends to help with the babies, sleeping over many nights. Before long, I managed to move in with her without Joe noticing the process?

Fortunately, he continued to pay my school fees at Saint Anthony High School, later changed to Trenton Catholic. From my aunt Jeannette's house, it took two buses and nearly two hours to get to school every morning, but I was never late. *Don't be discouraged,* I told myself. *This is a better arrangement for my overall sanity.*

Once I reached the proper age, Joe taught me how to drive, and eventually the blue car was finally mine. I became the envy of the other students. Every weekend, Joe came to get the car to fill it up with gas for the week and did a service check to ensure the car was safe to drive. All seemed to balance out; I had a surrogate mother in

Aunt Jeannette, and she was grateful for my support. Despite the difficulties and hardships we endured along the way, we stuck together like glue. To keep our family strong, we practiced teamwork. I stayed with Aunt Jeannette until Joe and she drove me to college.

Having to take the SAT test and applying to colleges arrived like a sudden flash of lightning. The sister who was my high school advisor held my hand every step of the way. She was fully aware that I had no one at home to help me get prepared for the test and navigate through the many application forms, so she took it as her personal mission to help me get into college. And that she did! We narrowed it down to two colleges in New Jersey. She thought it was best that I stay in the state and that the college be small in size, have a student population under five thousand, and have a suburban campus. Though she preferred the other campus, I wanted to be closer to home along the Northeast Corridor Train Line, so I could go home as needed.

I was accepted at all the universities to which I applied. Aunt Jeannette, Papa, and I celebrated this achievement with dinner at a nice restaurant. This triumph was all ours, and it could never be taken away from us. Our family was moving forward just as expected.

Time was spinning faster and faster. Graduation day soon arrived. Dressed in my white-and-gold robe, Papa, with Aunt Jeannette next to him, drove me to my commencement ceremony. I rushed to get in the line outside of

Stability | The Belle of the Ball

the Saint Anthony Church as they went to take their seats inside. To the sound of the organ playing the ceremonial graduation music, the procession made its way into the church. Passing by, I glanced over to find my father and my aunt Jeannette. They both wore broad smiles and had gleams in their eyes. He stood tall and proud. His dreams for me were being realized as I reached a major milestone in the form of high school graduation. It was an achievement that no one in our family had ever experienced. This was a victorious moment for the entire family.

Pursuing my educational dreams was beginning to become a reality; I had dared to rise above the oppressive culture from which I came. I knew that attending college would further alter my family history. I had been born in a country that offered little hope for a prosperous future and only the barest of basics—food, shelter, and little education. Had I remained in Haiti, I would never have moved our family out of poverty.

Haiti is my birth country, and I'll always hold its beauty close, but I instinctively knew I could be challenged more in my lifetime. The pressure of this generational shift was alive within me. I was on my way to being the first college graduate in my entire family lineage. Douglass College at Rutgers University was the college of my choice, and I was elated when I was accepted. Conviction in my heart for greater possibilities was strong. My next life chapter would reveal more about living in America as a young Haitian woman.

Preparation for college during the summer months was a priority, and before long, the day arrived. From Haiti to America, who would have projected a college experience for this young Haitian girl from *Lakou dis pieces*? Would it be everything I expected?

Papa and Aunt Jeannette drove me to the campus and helped me unpack and settle into my dormitory room. Their emotions were transparent, as evidenced by the flood of tears when they said goodbye. I suddenly realized what was happening—my journey toward pursuing a medical profession was becoming a reality. There I was, on campus. Progress is made!

I was eagerly looking forward to meeting my college roommates. Three of us girls had established friendships over the summer before arriving on campus. Our letters to each other consisted of common-interest topics and sharing of personal information. Innocently, we didn't include any mention of our ethnic backgrounds or race. After all, it was the late seventies—social media did not exist, and Googling wasn't possible.

Moving into a dormitory room was an entirely new experience. Sharing a living space with strangers felt odd. While back in Haiti, we did live several in a room, but those were close relations. This roommate situation was different. I had to be open to the college experience and moving in with two girls I had never met in person, but I welcomed this new living arrangement.

I was putting the final touches on my side of the room when both my roommates walked in. Smiling and giggling, they introduced themselves. No handshakes and no hugs.

"Hello, my name is Fannie," one said.

"And I am Katy," said the other.

"Nice to meet you finally. I am Marie."

"I see you came earlier. Did you visit the campus already?" I asked.

"Yes, I arrived in the morning," said Fannie, "and Katy arrived early afternoon. We just came back to pick up my jacket."

Before I could say another word, hastily, they both left within minutes for dinner, without any mention of my joining them. Immediately, my heart sank.

Weeks went by, and those two behaved as if they had known each other for years. They left every morning together for classes, and when Friday came, they both went home for the weekend.

Then there was the weekend that Katy did not go home. That's when I learned from Katy that Fannie had expressed concern about sharing a room with a Black person. Fannie was from a town farther north in New Jersey; it had next to zero people of color. My presence apparently was causing her a lot of discomfort.

I expressed my appreciation to Katy for explaining the situation. "How about you, Katy? How do you feel?" I asked her.

"I am not like her at all. I just try to be understanding towards her feelings, but she is completely out of line. I am glad I didn't go home this weekend, and I have a chance to get to know you."

As soon as Fannie returned to campus, though, Katy and Fannie went back to being inseparable. I soon recognized where Katy's loyalty lay.

A sense of not belonging anywhere seemed to creep into my world again, which reminded me of my first years in America. In elementary school, the students' nickname for me was Frenchie, and there were times when my meal ticket or other items that belonged to me were taken. Kids can be cruel, but I had a deeper purpose in life.

I began to analyze Fannie's thinking and how I felt about sharing a room with her. In Haiti, we only had the magnificent Blacks or the *mulats*,[15] who were the minorities. These girls were neither. I decided that their existence would not bother me a bit; I would not let anything curb my curiosity to learn more about different cultures. *Neither will this disappointment disrupt my college journey,* I told myself. This, to me, was just an introduction to the authentic face of racism in America. I decided that this revelation of outward ignorance would not immobilize me. My pursuit was greater than friendship.

College years were challenging. First, Father began having health issues; he suffered two heart attacks in a short time period. The first time, I was in the midst of finals, and I had to leave school to rush to his side. Acting more like his caretaker and mother, I was often the dutiful daughter he counted on; I was all that he had. I wasn't sure if I could stand it if he were gone, not after all I went through to stay afloat in America.

Sadly, my father's difficulties with his illnesses caused unemployment, which placed a financial burden on my shoulders. My mother and family in Haiti still needed support, and they depended on me to send money each month, which my father unwillingly took care of. But now I had to figure it out all on my own.

I did what I could with the money from financial-aid awards and part-time jobs. I learned how to borrow from Peter to pay Paul, and vice versa. I worked in the school cafeteria as a dishwasher and server. To earn additional income, I became a certified home health aide and provided care to the elderly in their homes. Any extra money, I sent home to Haiti. Being in school and trying to earn a degree did not spare me from my family obligations.

Finally, I secured the most interesting job working in the biochemistry department as a laboratory assistant, and, amazingly, it aligned with my coursework. In time, this significant introduction would foster a marriage of sorts. That was it. I found a science that I loved, and that science, the chemistry of life, found me!

Nevertheless, sending money to my family back home in Haiti was a responsibility on which I couldn't turn my back. Now a wage earner, this new adult challenge was critical, but I also needed to be a successful college student. At times, it caused me to question this burden. I had to pay my tuition and care for my personal needs, and looming in the background was Mama in Haiti. Worrying if they had clothes and supplies for school, whether or not their rent was paid, or if they had a meal every day weighed me down. It didn't seem fair, but I understood the nature of my life, and I was striving to do my best despite it all.

All I wanted was to graduate and secure employment so I could send for my mother. While others focused on their studies and social life, I was dealing with stressful family issues. The pressure of meeting the needs in all corners of my life was draining. I felt as if my energy resources were being used up. All the while, I was trying to live a reasonably normal life or, at the very least, *survive*.

Faith is a constant in my life. My religious background was instilled in me by Mama. *"God shows us the way,"* she *would say. "He understands our needs and will always carry us through troubled times."* I held on to that and found the power and strength to soldier on.

Developing friendships on campus didn't come easily. This feeling of thinking that I was not like others lurked in my mind. I learned to reject those thoughts and focus on the end goal, which was earning a college degree.

Willa, an upperclassman and my college-dorm neighbor, was enchanted by love and mature beyond her years. As coworkers in the dining hall, we walked home after work together, so we spent hours cultivating a friendship. Neither of us ever had an issue with our races being different, so our relationship blossomed going forward. Having Willa as a friend gave me a sense of belonging, something that was lacking with my roommates.

Later in the semester, I met her fiancé, a French gentleman named Théo, who had already completed his degree. His frequent visits to drop off Willa presented me with chances to practice my French that I was beginning to forget.

Willa graduated, but our friendship didn't end there. She surprised me with an invitation to her wedding to Théo. That beautiful spring day in May, Aunt Jeannette and I dressed in our best outfits and attended a most beautiful wedding ceremony held in a small white church in a rural town in New Jersey.

The next semester brought new opportunities to make new friends. At an international students' cultural event on campus, I met Teeloo and Hanaya, who were fascinating, proud African Americans. They donned authentic, African-colored clothing—vibrant reds, blacks, and greens—with head wraps and natural hair to complete their fashion statements. With utmost loyalty to the African culture, upon their return from a tour of East Africa, they took on new names that represented them best. *"Can you believe our parents chose actual European names for us?!"* Teeloo once exclaimed.

The more our friendships evolved, the more fascinated I was becoming with them and their love for Mama Africa. At the same time, I admired their bravery in exposing their authentic selves, day in and day out, regardless of what other students may think. I had a homeland with its own unique culture, too, but that connection seemed to begin drifting out of my life. My only connection to Haiti during those college years was my mother in the form of letters I periodically received from her. Observing their genuine respect for the African culture reminded me there was a void in my life; I missed my Haitian heritage. And I missed my mother even more.

Spending time with Teeloo and Hanaya renewed my love for my culture. They both lived in what was known as the Africana House, which gradually became my home, too. I decided that this group of culturally energetic souls suited my lifestyle, so I moved in. Sharing a room with Teeloo gave me a sense of belonging and made me feel that it was acceptable for me to be a Haitian Creole outside of my family setting. The residents of the Africana House became my college family. Sometimes they called me by my adored nickname, *TiFoune*, which they heard my father utter once when he came to pick me up. Finally, I belonged. This African family of college students lent me their heritage, and I was utterly embracing all of it—the culture, the people…and in time an older foreign student from West Africa who would soon attempt to claim his space in my life.

Jay was much more sophisticated than the other college students. Ten years older than most, he zoned in on me just as an eagle spots its prey. Because he was a lot older, I had to think twice about considering any type of relationship that could evolve. After all, my father had laid out the guidelines for my life. Dating, falling in love, and getting married were not parts of the plan for becoming a doctor. However, I was eager to lean on someone, especially since my father was sickly, and I longed for someone to take the lead.

With his ebony skin, well-sculpted seventies Afro, dominant stature, and all the qualities of a strong, well-groomed gentleman, he indeed impressed me. Here was someone who was attentive, caring, and offered support when needed. Instantly, I intuited Jay's place in my life. He was forward, protective, confident, and worldly. Always a step ahead of me, he often went out of his way to ease the burdens that impacted my life.

Coming back to school one evening, I grabbed my book bag and quickly exited the train. Instantly, I was thinking, *Should I walk it, wait for the bus, or take a taxi to my dorm?* Pondering what to do, I looked ahead to find Jay standing at the station, sporting his signature broad smile. *How did he know that I would be arriving on the train right now? I wondered.*

"Hi, Jay, what are you doing here? Are you going somewhere?"

"I came to pick you up, of course."

"Well, that's so kind of you and perfect timing!"

"I thought so."

"Wait, how did you know my train would arrive at this time?"

"That's right; I didn't know because you didn't tell me when you were coming back."

"Interesting."

"Well, since the trains run by the hour, I've come by each hour since early afternoon to see if you were on it. I knew eventually you would come back to school."

"Even more interesting."

"Let's get in the car. I'll drop you off at your dorm."

I was thankful for this gesture and for having someone care about my well-being.

Then there was the time when I was at the library, preparing for an exam. I looked up and saw him walking toward my desk with a smile bigger than usual.

"Hi, Jay!"

"I stopped to get the key to your room."

"The key to my room? Why?"

"To drop off some fish for you. You can have that when you return from the library."

Cleverly, he borrowed the key to my dorm room to hook up a stereo system that he'd bought me. Imagine my surprise when I walked into my room to the sound of Haitian Kompa[16] music. I quickly called Jay for an explanation.

"I just want you to have music from home to listen to," he said.

Each time Jay made a kind gesture, my feelings for him developed further, and I clung to him more and more, but cautiously. Sharing my story with Jay about coming to America, leaving my family behind, and then dealing with Papa's illnesses unloaded the emotional weight I had been carrying for years. These stories you just don't share with other students. But I told Jay how I yearned to see my mother and that I planned to send for her after graduation. I wanted my mother more than anything.

Jay heard my heart, and before long, he came up with an idea. Though I was skeptical, he joined my mission to find a way for my mother to come to America and attend my graduation. *"I will compose a written plea requesting that your mother obtain a visa so that she can participate in the graduation ceremony."*

Someone was finally in my corner, helping me bring my mother to America. While Jay was writing the letter, I rushed to the office to ask for the family invitations. Little did they know that one of those invitations was about to change my life for the better. Later that day, I eagerly telephoned my mother to share the latest ideas about her coming to America.

"Hello, pitit mouin, I am happy to hear from you."

"Mama, go and apply for a passport immediately. You must hurry because we are running out of time. My friend and I are working on a plan, and as soon as all the necessary documents are in place, there is a chance you may leave Haiti for America."

"Are you serious, my daughter? I will call back to let you know when I can get the passport. I'll bring extra money with me in case it looks like it may take longer, if you know what I mean."

"Go, Mama. Talk to you soon."

Later, Jay brought over his letter. The document opened with a formal salutation and continued with an appeal to reunite a mother with her daughter on graduation day. It was so eloquently written that I instantly began to appreciate Jay's level of intelligence. The letter and the formal college-graduation invitation were sent to the United States Embassy in Port-Au-Prince. For the first time in a long while, I felt my life could be whole again.

I deserve this miracle. Why not me? But then again, why me? I am just another immigrant, among many living in America, yearning to reunite with her family. Surely, God will grant me this one.

Chapter 10
Reunited with Mama

Good Things Do Happen

With bated breath, I waited…and waited…and waited to hear the results of the embassy visit. With one phone call, our lives could change forever.

"Mama, how'd it go? Did they approve your visa? Please tell me."

"TiFoune…" and then a pause.

My nerves were frazzled. I couldn't wait any longer. "Mama!" I screamed into the phone.

"Yes, yes! God is good! I'm coming to America!" She continued to speak, but what I heard was a cacophony of sound. It took me some time to dissect the conversation as she related how she had spent the night before on her knees, praying to God for deliverance. Her prayers were miraculously answered with a five-year passport stamp granting her a multiple-entry visa. With that, she was on her way to see her daughter, a young woman now in her twenties and a soon-to-be college graduate.

All of our efforts paid off. My mother was granted a visa that made it possible for her to land gracefully into my life just before college graduation. Anticipating this ceremonial stepping stone, I believed that, from there on, anything was possible. There was nothing I couldn't achieve. Planning her arrival fueled me with empowerment and a belief that I could make *anything* happen. I was in charge of my life and ready to discover its unfolding. Mama was finally coming to America.

Words can't describe my state of anticipation at being reunited with my mother. I was more than thrilled; I was feeling the blessing of the moment in all my bones. Good things really do happen in due time.

I kept my composure long enough to say goodbye, and I ran back to my room in awe and disbelief. Feeling weak in the knees, I dropped onto my bed as if a load I had been carrying for so long had totally disintegrated. Mama would finally see all that I had accomplished. Thanks to Jay, who wrote that amazing letter and convinced me that the plan would work.

Challenges never cease to poke my world. I was on to the next worries. *Now, what about the plane ticket? And where will Mama live? I asked myself.*

Even though my father wasn't emotionally attached to my mother throughout the years, I never expected their relationship to dissolve, but it did. Unfortunately, this is the fate of most immigrant families when they are forced to separate. So how could I persuade Papa to help with buying plane tickets? And I didn't think Mama could stay with him, either. That was another issue. I had to worry about the plane tickets first.

It was time to take a train ride home.

"Papa, great news! I did it. You said I had to figure it out, and guess what? I did!"

"You did what?"

"Well, guess!"

"You know I don't like to play games. What do have to say?"

"Mama is coming. She was granted a visa to attend my graduation, and now it's just a matter of buying plane tickets."

"So?"

"So-o? I need money for the roundtrip tickets. You know I have no money."

"You want *me* to give you the money?" Pause. "I think not."

"Papa, you better stop before I start to tickle you. You know how you hate being happy!"

His teasing and taunting almost broke me, but I held my ground in an amicable way. I stared into his eyes, though with a look that said, *"Don't annoy me, dude!"*

"All right, all right. I always knew you could do it. I'm proud of you, by the way, *TiFoune*."

I had no time for his flattery. There was more to do.

In the end, he handled the travel arrangements. I was relieved. My affection for him was restored in some way. The purchase of the tickets by my father was a load off my shoulders. He came through and did his part to reunite me with Mama, and that's what mattered most. I felt a shift in my heart for the better. Even though our father-daughter relationship suffered from this betrayal—not bringing Mother over sooner—our family bond was not completely severed.

Now…who will provide the affidavit of support to be her host? My father's younger brother, the pastor, maybe?

I went straight to his house to share the good news with him. He, too, smiled proudly.

"Uncle," I continued, "the embassy asked for someone to take financial responsibility for Mama during her stay. Will you do this for me?"

"After all that you did to make this happen? Of course, my dear TiFoune. I will fill out the forms."

"Thank you, Uncle."

Now, where will Mama really live?

I was living off campus, renting a room in a house with other students. I had to make a bold decision. She would live with me. That was the only solution at the time.

The day finally arrived! Going to the airport to pick up my mother was history in the making.

A young Haitian girl of thirteen comes to America to change her life. She lives with a father she barely knows, enters the American school system, and assimilates on schedule. She enters college and graduates, then is reunited with her mother.

I played this recording in my head for years, as if an outside entity were planning my life, and I was the star performer. I didn't make these choices for my life. If anything, my parents did. *How will it all turn out? Do they really know what is best for me?* These emotions and unanswered questions lingered within me time and again.

Fortunately, Jay offered to drive me to John F. Kennedy Airport. We arrived early. Expectedly, my stomach was acting up. Was I nervous or hungry? What if they questioned my mother at the Immigrations counter, and she couldn't communicate? *Worse yet, what if she was sent back to Haiti?* My stomach was twisted in knots. Food is definitely my companion when it comes to calming me down, but I wasn't giving in. I would save my appetite and celebrate later with Mama. Jay was planning to take us out for a festive meal to welcome her long-awaited arrival. Everything was planned.

We parked the car, and suddenly it hit me. It was over six years since I had last seen my mother when I was sixteen years old. I had waited so long for this moment, this masterful performance , and it was finally here. I felt genuinely blessed. I kept thanking Jay for the role he played in the execution of our plan.

At the terminal, people gathered around the waiting area with expressions of giddiness. In airports, most people waiting for their parties to arrive are in good spirits, and I was certainly one of them. Twenty minutes passed before passengers started arriving. As I moved my head from side to side, looking past everyone, I tried to cast my eyes on my mother as soon as she walked within sight. My mind chased the unimaginable—*What if Immigrations stops her? What if the plan flops? What if she gives the wrong answer? What if…?*

Can my big wish really come true?

Then, suddenly among the crowd, flowing like a swan, I saw my mother pushing her cart. Time stopped as she walked towards me. She stood out in her stylish teal dress that I had sent her, high-heeled shoes, and the biggest smile I've ever seen. Her dark-auburn hair was neatly coiffed. I immediately noticed that the years had taken nothing from her; she appeared ageless. Her expression exemplified a decade of stored hope and longing. I could see her glowing, cocoa-brown skin beaming.

Her voice dominated the noise of the airport crowd. She squealed out loud. "There you are! TiFoune, TiFoune!"

When my eyes met hers, I felt victorious. *I succeeded!*

"Oh, look at you, my baby girl. You are all grown up!"

With a wholehearted hug, tears of joy streaming down, she embraced me tightly. It was as if she were a mother greeting her newborn child, except I was now twenty-two. She held me with such tight force. It was as if her loving strength had kidnapped my body. Even though I was ecstatic, my hug back couldn't compete. I let her hug me until she'd had enough.

Then, for the first time, I began to think about what her emotional journey must have been like. While I was in America, managing my life, she was waiting in the wings for her turn. Her only daughter was across the Caribbean and growing up without her. Our experiences were the same, in that we missed each other, but different because I was building my future, while she had just been waiting. Suddenly it came to me how connected we truly were on that journey.

When we pulled away from each other, I caught her eyes and captured the impact of the moment; the emotional pull of our reunion was an intense realm of personal growth. In my mind, I could hear her saying, *"We did it, TiFoune! It wasn't easy for you or me, but we won the battle! Your mama is here now."*

Immigrants come to America every day, hoping to create a promising future. Some make it. Some don't. But at that moment, all that mattered was my mother's love. Whether or not I made it was in the hands of destiny. Then and there, I was filled with joy. Now I, too, had someone to call Mama in America.

I introduced her to Jay, the one who had stepped into my life to orchestrate this miracle with me. I told her we had put our heads together and made this moment possible. She grabbed him abruptly and gave him a deserving, grateful hug.

With a broad smile, he grabbed the suitcase off the cart and said, "Let's go home and celebrate."

But where is home? I pondered. *Do not worry your little head,* I thought to myself. *We are going home to my Off-Campus room at Douglass College, Rutgers University; however odd that might seem.*

Chatting with Mama in Creole felt as if I were home again. For the past several years, our mode of communication had been limited to exchanging letters. There were times that we indulged in lengthy phone calls, but those were rare. Now we could talk for hours and hours.

With all the excitement of Mama's arrival and my impending graduation, the thought of convincing my father to welcome my mother into his home had escaped my mind. So she moved in with me. We really had no other choice. It was the final semester, so her stay with me would be brief.

While I focused on my finals, Jay brought groceries to us, and Mama made use of the shared kitchen. As unusual as it was, the other students accepted the situation.

My only regret was not participating in my college graduation ceremony. The finale of this monumental family-legacy event got lost in the task of getting Mama to America. That was the priority. So graduation day came and went. I had my mom. What could top that?

Everything in my life was coming together. I obtained a college degree and reunited with my mother. At twenty-two, life was moving faster than I could handle it, and I was more than ready for the ride, except for one thing. I knew that medical school would not be part of my life plan. I had achieved part of what my father expected: I graduated from college in America—with a bachelor's degree in biochemistry, no less—the first in the Michaud family tree to be college educated.

Somewhere along the line, I had decided to take another path, even though I secretly knew that would crush my father's dream. In his mind, being a doctor represented success for our Haitian lineage; it was a significant win for the family, as well as for the villagers back in the mountains of Trouin. Changing my direction could risk damaging our father-daughter relationship. But if I lived someone else's dream, I would risk damaging my relationship with myself.

Chapter 11
Claiming Me

"Mediocre, that will be your middle name. If you decide not to be a doctor, that's what you are—MEDIOCRE!" Those words from my father almost shattered my self-worth and spoiled the hope in my heart I had for myself.

"Joe, let's be serious for a minute," I said firmly, looking him straight in the eyes. "How do you think I could compete with other premed students with everything that I have on my plate?" I asked in my defense.

He remained silent.

My rant continued, "Do you realize that everyone has done their best to survive in this surreal space that you placed us in for the past decade? Had my mother been here all along, you could have realized your dream. But you chose to do otherwise."

I paused briefly.

"And now that I've graduated from college, it would be the perfect time to prepare for the next step to go to medical school. But I can bet you other young graduates are not looking for a home for their mother to stay in. Until I get a job so that I can get my own apartment, I am also homeless."

Having said my peace, I left my father's home. I was on my way to becoming the strong, self-possessed, accomplished young woman with dreams of creating my life, my way. I refused to let him shun me and break my spirit. My father and I were two separate people—what he wanted for me and what I wanted for myself were different. My life had to be owned and directed by me from now on; this is what I knew in my heart. I decided to stop living up to his expectations. I had earned a college degree and brought my mother from Haiti. Now I was in charge of my future.

Next on the agenda was to choose a career path, or would a career pick me? Part of me wasn't sure where I was headed, or even if I was going anywhere, but the leader in me guided my footsteps. One thing was certain—I needed to support my new family: my mother and me. A steady paycheck as a stability analyst in a pharmaceutical laboratory provided that much-needed stability in my life. But I still had to supplement my income.

A free facial would lead me to the world of Mary Kay cosmetics. I found my niche—the world of science, cosmetics, and beauty. Working for Mary Kay as an independent consultant afforded me the opportunity to learn skills I would have never learned in college. The cosmetic business caught my interest, and my marketing and sales side was born. Before long, I was earning an income through my sales and commissions that, combined, surpassed the amount of my *steady job's paycheck*.

From the onset of my association with Mary Kay, I diligently followed the blueprint of their training program and worked my way up to become one of the top performers in my unit. Climbing their *ladder of success* was an arduous journey. All the hard work I invested paid off, and I became a sales director, which earned me the famous Mary Kay *pink* car.

Pink elements were scattered throughout my life. Even Mama's favorite color was pink. And with Mary Kay, pink was showing its face in my life again. Driving down the street, the wind blowing in my hair, I sang that "Pink Cadillac" song. I was one of Mary Kay's youngest sales directors. I was earning awards—diamond jewelry—and going to her pink house in Dallas, Mary Kay herself the hostess. It was all so exhilarating. It was the beginning of my newfound career as a businesswoman in the world of cosmetics.

My full-time position was soon in the distant past. Life moved forward, and thoughts of marriage and a family sent me into a trance. I wanted that dream. The entire fairy tale in which *he* snatches me away in awe of my Creole beauty and many talents, and then I am granted my happily ever after. A scene right out of a movie, and I was the star.

Well, *he* did arrive, and *he* did sweep me off my feet. My relationship with Jay offered me that dream. Leaning on someone after all the years of others relying on my support was comforting. He never gave up on me. He understood I had many obligations and patiently waited.

So when he proposed marriage, I decided to say yes in the midst of everything. My father was not pleased with my decision and refused to walk me down the aisle. That was Joe being Joe. I didn't understand his reasoning but I knew he loved me. He wanted me to further my education to become a doctor and didn't accept my choice to marry. My godfather would be his replacement on my wedding day. My mother, on the other hand, envisioned grandchildren. In her eyes, at twenty-five I was now married and ready for the next part of my life.

Jay supported my role as a Mary Kay businesswoman; without him, I don't think I could have achieved the level of success I did. He was a faithful Mary Kay husband. Jay worked full-time at the telephone company—and tirelessly worked to improve our weekly Mary Kay sales revenues. His client list exceeded mine at times. To acknowledge his monthly sales achievements, I awarded him the use of our pink car to drive to his workplace. He gladly breezed down the streets and enjoyed the attention when people turned their heads to see a man driving a pink car.

All the while, Jay still had not completed his college degree because he was only attending part-time. So as a married couple, we decided that it was best for him to become a full-time student. Once he earned his bachelor's, he could move on to gain his master's, then become a certified public accountant, which would benefit our family in the long term.

As life happened, we were about to become parents. Careerwise, my life was on track at the time, but being pregnant redirected my goals. I was a Mary Kay director, and traveling around the city and the country, constantly on the go, was a part of my lifestyle. I was forced to reprioritize if I wanted a healthy baby. Several months into the pregnancy, some danger signs forced me to become bedridden. Nearing the end of my pregnancy, but not quite full-term, my water broke, and I was rushed to the hospital. Devastating fear held my heart hostage.

While my mother stayed home to prepare the house for the baby, Jay was by my side in the hospital. Periodically, he reported my progress to my mother. Since I knew that the baby would be a boy, I felt some anxiety because I hadn't told Jay yet. He desperately wanted a girl; her name was predetermined. Thinking about this now, it seems comical, but at the time, I was worried that Jay wouldn't accept a son. I was wrong.

"How can I ever be so fortunate?" he muttered when he saw his newborn son, and my worries disappeared. Jay fell instantly in love with his son—as if all thoughts of a little girl had left his mind, and I was as proud as any new mother.

Our son was named after an uncle on his father's side, a supreme court justice in Ghana. His middle name was his tribal name and an honorable tribute to his Ghanaian heritage. Once they saw his middle name, staff at the hospital raved about this newborn who had family roots in the Gold Coast. The nurses adored and fussed over him. He was their lone Black star.

Marriage was an unusual world for me. I didn't have a proper model of a marriage partnership growing up. My parents underwent that forced separation with my father's emigration to America. I was nine years old when that occurred. After that, I lived with each parent individually. So I never knew of the marriage concept and probably wasn't ready or able to maintain such an intimate relationship. Jay was a good man. He provided financially, cared for us, and he took the lead. More than anything, he was almost a father figure in my life, and I thought our relationship was more like that of a father and daughter.

Since my mother lived with us, she fulfilled my needs regarding childcare. As time passed, my relationship with my mother became dominant in the household. Soon my closeness to my mother took precedence over my relationship with Jay. As a new mom, I relied on her more and more. Slowly, the marriage began to dissolve. Although I was gifted with motherhood, I knew losing Jay as my partner would weigh on my heart and conscience.

How did we get to this place? Why can't we make our marriage work, if only for the sake of our son? What growth can I take from this experience?

I was a proud mother of an adorable, energetic baby boy, and he was my strength. At the same time, I found it difficult to pick up where I had left off in my business, so finding a new path and reclaiming *me* became my personal life goal. My role as the head of the family came with making decisions about which I was clueless, but I was determined to find a way.

Chapter 12
More Life and More Roles

A Life of Discovery

Education was the primary reason that I came to America. As embarrassing as it is to say, my father was right. A bachelor's degree wasn't enough to secure a profession that would amount to financial success. I decided to go back to school.

Fortunately, my mother lived with me, and her support was undeniably crucial. We had both grown from all of the experiences, and I soon learned that our mother-daughter bond was of great value, more than I would have ever thought.

My mother's assistance christened every part of my world. Without her, my professional pursuit of adding to my repertoire of credentials would have taken longer to achieve, and quite possibly would have failed. Back in Haiti, she helped raise her grandchildren, several orphans, and that infant girl, all of whom were unexpectedly brought into her home. Being a mother is a role she adored. Now she offered her hands-on mothering to my family.

Fairleigh Dickson University, roughly an hour and a half away from my home, offered a master's program in cosmetics science. I enrolled. Combining my skills and experience would help me reach another level in my career. Fortunately, my employer was flexible with my schedule and made my commute much more bearable. As a young mother, a student, and a working professional, this gesture meant the world to me and my family.

Attending the master's program pushed me toward learning more about who I was, what I wanted to achieve, and how I could create a promising future for myself. My father's voice was in the back of my mind. Hearing his echoing words—*"TiFoune, education is essential; education is critical."*—directed my course of action and held me captive. I needed his declaration of approval. In my heart, my motive was to prove him right. I could be a successful Haitian-born female who came to America to live out her dreams. Still, my journey was just beginning, and I had a long way to go.

Now in my thirties, the caring mother of a young son, I had a thirst and hunger for an exciting future. I was ready to dictate my career using my own designed plan, independent of what my father wanted for me. I was on the move for more life, more roles, and more opportunities.

While I was managing my next life plan, my father's health slipped. Between his unhealthy lifestyle and heart condition, his future looked grim. He insisted on having his own place and absolutely refused to live with me so that my mother and I could keep an eye on him. He always had that stubborn pride. I visited him as often as possible, but my roles were many, and my responsibilities absorbed my time. As much as possible, I went to him and did what was needed. Occasionally, my mother went to his place to cook and do some chores.

After many close calls, he passed away in his early sixties, right before Christmas. The day of his funeral was a sad and solemn day in my life. It was a difficult goodbye. I watched my mother weep. For her, it was an ambiguous loss. She lost the love that really wasn't. Or was it? My father was a complicated individual.

As I got older, I developed a greater understanding of my father's struggles. He left a caste system in Haiti, where people had great admiration for people of lighter skin pigmentation. He landed in America in the height of the Civil Rights Movement of the sixties. For these reasons, and those happening inside his head, he believed that he wasn't worthy of my mother's love. He lived with this inferiority complex, believing his dark skin made him less desirable in my mother's eyes.

My father, who brought me to America to change the family legacy, would forever be painfully out of the picture. The man, the icon who embodied the driving force for the success I would achieve in life, would no longer be around. Even though I didn't become a medical doctor, he left with his heart happy as his only daughter became a college graduate, and he lived to see his first grandson. Who was I without Joe's demands on my life? I would learn in time.

Family is important to me, especially since my own childhood lacked what I longed for: a mother and father who raised children in one home. Attempting marriage again wasn't something I had on my mind or calendar, but it showed up without warning, so I surrendered any uncertainties and greeted love at the door.

My second husband, Ron, was of true Haitian background—born and raised there most of his life. We met at a barbershop, of all places. I was taking my son for a routine haircut. While waiting our turn, I overheard a conversation about France and turned my head to see a well-dressed man wearing sharply creased black pants and a freshly ironed white shirt. Since I had traveled to France to visit family, I joined in on the conversation. While waiting our turn, the chitchat grew personal, and I learned about his recent move to America and heard about his aspirations of journeying toward a better life. The kinship was set. Dreamer one met dreamer two. And meeting someone connected to my heritage closed the gap in my sense of belonging; it was strangely familiar, almost nostalgic. When I left the barbershop that afternoon, I felt a sense of connection to this French stranger.

If my father were alive, would he approve? Why am I always thinking about what my father wanted? Attachment to his approval hijacks my senses because I have an emotional arrangement inside—please my father, and my world is all right.

One date with Ron turned into two and three, and a committed relationship was established. Our Haitian backgrounds felt like home to me—the home that existed in my heart and soul, the home that I left at thirteen years old. My inner longing for the past somehow showed up in Ron, and I felt satisfied and settled with him by my side. More time passed, and we grew enamored with each other, then decided to marry.

Ella, my second child and my first girl, was born seven years after her brother. The pregnancy was perfect and predictable. Her untamed bush of hair at birth clarified that she would need complete girl attention, which I couldn't wait for. Having had a son for so many years, I welcomed my little girl. One son and one daughter were ideal. Ella's godmother, who lived in France, sent pastel-colored dresses in a signature smock style in which the princesses and princes of Europe were adorned; we dressed her like a store-bought doll. She was a true princess.

Motherhood couldn't have been better; this was one of the happiest years of my life. My oldest child's big-brother status left him proud, too. As the big brother, his role was that of both bodyguard and playmate. He was so protective of his baby sister that if I left home and Ella in Ron's care, I trusted that she would be watched with extra-loving care if her big brother was there. Ella's birth gave me a little girl and my son a sibling. Marriage and motherhood nurtured my need for a family.

In time, I got more than my share of family. To my surprise, another blessing was on its way, so my mother's living with me was everything I could ask for. However, during this pregnancy, I was faced with losing my job—a sudden downsize. To add to this stress, I developed health issues. Fortunately, I gave birth to a healthy baby girl. We all had more to fuss over—Jolia. She was as cute as she could be.

My mother was in grandmother heaven with the two girls under her wings to care for while she showered the firstborn with the love and attention because he was accustomed to being an only child. With only a year between my two daughters, the household mirrored chaos. But my immense joy would soon be shattered.

All kids have distinctive personalities, and, naturally, they develop in their own time. Still, Ella showed signs of indifference that I didn't experience with my other children. She didn't seem to respond when we called her name. At first, we joked that she was angry because the new baby took the attention from her. Ella enjoyed dancing to the catchy jingles of TV commercials, so I witnessed her responding to sound. This meant that her hearing was intact. Still, I knew something was not right. Several doctor visits later, I was informed that my daughter was on the spectrum.

"What is that supposed to mean?" I asked the doctor.

"Well, the diagnosis is PDD-NOS, pervasive developmental disorder, not otherwise specified," she replied.

Great. The doctor spelled it out, but what those words meant for my daughter, I was yet to find out. Initially, the diagnosis perturbed me because I hadn't expected to hear that my child may have developmental disabilities, and I wasn't intellectually prepared to know what to do. My concerns grew as I discovered more about how autism manifests itself. Would she be on the high-functioning end of the autism spectrum and have full capabilities to learn, or not?

In time, I did what any parent would do. I faced it head-on and began my research to learn about autism. Acceptance of the unexpected goes a long way. Throughout her growing years, advocating for my daughter was another add-on to my parenting responsibilities.

My daughter's awareness of her disability helped her to protect herself against others whose understanding was limited. While some students turned to bullying tactics, she learned to stand up for herself. During those turbulent middle school years, she challenged those bullies in school and sheltered others when help was nowhere to be found. With these struggles, she was prone to depression which required support from the family. Resources gained from my research about autism helped her to progress and eventually graduate from high school. Today, her high IQ allows her to engage in many different interests; she enjoys painting, culinary arts, anime, and graphic design, which supports her inner creativity. We even got her into college.

In the meanwhile, my relationship with Ron, which had begun with sincere intentions, began to suffer from a clash of cultures that soon knocked on our marriage door, and we had difficulties living through what seemed like conventional differences. For years, I embraced so much responsibility that when I intuited a shift in our marriage, I accepted the role of the leader in my life. I sensed I would soon be a single parent again. I did not know what the future would bring, but I was confident that I would do my best to handle it.

Divorce number two landed in my life; marriage didn't know my name. I thought this would carve me into a defeated position and destroy any hopes of my growing into the best me. The only thing I knew to do was move forward. So I worked diligently as a student, an employee, and a parent. I faced what I created and owned up to my part, knowing that the road ahead would not have an absence of struggles. By then, I had experienced two marriages, two divorces, single parenthood, academic life, and nurturing a child with a disability, all while being a career-driven woman of the world. Through these experiences, I had evolved from having an incredulous and second-guessing mindset to being a self-assured woman. I could handle whatever came my way. If life was testing me, I would stand ready to pass the test.

Next, unbeknownst to me, the *American dream* was on its way into my life. It was an ordinary Saturday with the usual errands to run. Dropping the girls off at their soccer game was my next task when the phone rang. I could never have predicted the next turn of events.

"Hello, Reeta, is all well?"

"Yes, Marie, how is the family?"

"We're doing well."

"Marie, I have to talk to you about the townhouse."

"Is there a problem?"

"No, not at all, Marie. Dr. Rekogi and I decided the time has come to list the rental property for sale. The real estate market is expected to drop sharply, and we must move fast."

At the time, I had been renting a townhome from Reeta, its owner, for nearly six years. Our relationship worked, and I loved living in this spacious home in New Jersey. I had no plan to move anytime soon. I dreaded another life change.

"Would you be interested in buying the house, Marie?"

"Oh." I hesitated. Gears were shifting, and I had to think fast.

"You see, I wanted to offer you the first right of refusal. I'll offer you a good price, and we won't use agents in order to keep the closing costs very low."

It was easier to let her speak. My mind was racing uncontrollably. *I can't leave this school district. Have I failed my family? How can I share this news with the family?* My second marriage had just ended, so purchasing a home wasn't in the cards. This was bigger than I. *How can I handle this?*

"Was that the Rekogis, TiFoune?" my mother asked.

"Yes, it was."

"Are they coming down for something?"

"No, they only had a few questions. All is good," I replied and said nothing else.

The next day I got out of bed, resolved to make things happen. I did not know what yet, but an aggressive plan was needed. Back to the drawing board—I needed to learn about home buying and fast. At the same time, I had to look for a new rental in the same school district as a backup plan.

Soon I learned that it was possible to make a withdrawal without penalty against my IRA for a home purchase. For advice, I reached out to the village—my uncle, who just purchased his new home; his mortgage broker; my best friend, Mrs. Lite; and the president of my company. When I confided in my employer about this impending purchase, his support was in the form of an increase in salary; this was more fortune than I could handle. With everyone's support, I was able to make a large payment on my student loan to reduce my income-to-debt ratio. To say that my circle was there for me would be an understatement.

With ambition at its peak, I worked through each detail, waited out the process, and dared to dream outside of the box from which I had come—my birthplace, the long-forgotten Haitian village where people lived in a community of quiet desperation and deprivation. This was my history, my backstory, my destiny at one time in the distant past. Somehow, however, my parents had a vision for me that was better. And now the vision of having the security of a home for all of us was within reach—the American dream, as we know it.

Through hoops and loops and many acrobatic moves of the brain, I was able to buy my first home. The day of the closing was dreamlike. I was there by myself, my attorney by my side, signing one by one the myriad documents, as I became the owner of a three-bedroom townhouse in a suburban neighborhood, a permanent home in which to raise my growing family. I couldn't wait to get home. I burst through the door and found Mama waiting anxiously, her index finger on her lips.

"I got the key," I screamed. "This house is now ours." No other words were required.

Mama dropped to her knees to thank God for his favors and to pray for everyone who helped make this moment possible for our family.

Challenges like this were made for me; conquests breed more conquests and breathe empowerment into lives. I realized that I was living in an *all-American, dreamlike,* affluent community with people who had the same dream: live the white-picket-fence life in America. Truth be told, I was a Black, single mother of Caribbean descent, and my journey was different. Full realization of the dream would not be easy. Having experienced my first success on the road to the American dream, I decided, at the next opportunity, I would take action on my own terms.

Some years later, a larger home to accommodate my family in the same neighborhood complex became available. I was interested. This time, I wasn't under pressure to buy. I had the power of information at my fingertips. The neighborhood realtor found a tenant for my first property, and we happily moved into our new home. I turned a corner; I became a landlady.

Challenges are meant to teach you. So, the next few years, that's precisely what happened. My divorce taught me that I was a woman of resourceful means, but at the same time, society and friends were whispering in my ears that I needed a partner. That part of my life I couldn't quite figure out. No one seemed to have that perfect alignment, and after several trials, I gave up. I had learned by now that every relationship came with a price, and there were layers of discovery afterward. I had a legacy I wanted to fulfill, but it seemed more challenging with a partner. Despite failing at marriage, cultivating an amicable relationship with my children's father was the priority, and vital to lessening the anxiety that comes with divorce.

Our family of five, including Mama, made our home the center of ongoing activity. Raising three children, working full-time, and attending school controlled my calendar. Invigorating as this time of my life was, I needed to figure out where I was headed. Leaders need self-confidence and a clear vision, but each day was overwhelming, leaving me weakened and worn.

Without a doubt, I was grateful for my mother. She was the *poto mitan — the load-bearing pillar in a sacred temple*. The motherly and grandmotherly support she bestowed upon the family provided the strong foundation we all needed.

Chapter 13

Career Choices and More

Life Goes On

The more I became involved in the cosmetics industry, the more aligned I felt. When I learned about the Society of Cosmetic Chemists (SCC), I joined as a member and was assigned to the New York chapter. There are nineteen chapters under the umbrella of the national association. Education is the core of the SCC.

The society's mission is grounded in educating its members to advance cosmetic science. An adjunct professor of the cosmetic science master's program at Fairleigh Dickinson University (FDU) recommended that I volunteer with the New York chapter. There I was, at the Meadowlands Exposition Center, happily checking attendees in at my very first NYSCC Suppliers' Day trade show. From that first day, traveling to trade shows has become part of my professional life.

It was a normal workday, and a call came in while I was in the office. It was for me, and I picked up the phone.

"Hello."

"Hello, Marie, I am the chairman of the New York Chapter of the Society of Cosmetic Chemists (NYSCC). I have heard a lot about you."

"Great talking to you."

"Well, Marie, one of our committees has an open position. I would like to offer it to you."

With those words, I accepted my first position to chair the fellowship committee, with the responsibility of guiding new members joining the chapter. My professional and personal goals were aligning. My industry of choice was cosmetics, my profession was business development, and my expertise was cosmetic science. Offering my time and services to an organization whose mission is deeply rooted in education was a responsibility that I took seriously. And, of course, I had to feed my innermost mission of continuing my education in all areas of my life, hence the reason I offered my time, skills, and passion to help shape the cosmetics industry. Secretly, I knew my father would be as proud as I was.

Networking with other professionals while advancing my knowledge in the industry was nourishment in and of itself. Next was the opportunity to lead the house committee that manages the planning for the mandatory monthly educational meetings. Before long, public relations, which engages with industry trade journals and media companies, made its way to me. My circle was growing, I was acquiring new skills, and I was making a difference.

Meanwhile, traveling to meet customers at their locations and participating in training, trade shows, and conferences became a constant to fulfill work requirements. These travels offered me the opportunity to meet other decision-makers and inspirational professionals within the industry. Before you know it, my career was exhilarating in every sense of the word. Coming from a background of deprivation, both economically and educationally, I could hear my father's forceful voice loudly in my head, insisting that learning was the backbone of success. *"You can't learn without doing,"* he would say. I accepted and sought it all.

While my volunteering roles provided more opportunities to gain and display my leadership skills, a certification in small business and entrepreneurial studies was my next stepping stone. It was time to apply all I'd learned to one project.

First, I gathered the kids and their grandma for a family meeting to share my new endeavor. "Okay, everyone, attention, please, attention."

"Here we go again. What is it now, Mom?" said Jolia.

"After careful study of the market…and crafting a business plan," I enunciated in a deep voice, moving around as if presenting to a group, "I want to start my own business."

"That's a bold move," said Ella. "You are the boss, Mom."

"And"—I scratched my throat a couple of times—"can anybody guess what the name of the company will be?"

"Um, 1804, right?" said my son playfully.

Knowing exactly that he was referencing the year Haiti claimed its independence, I gave him the side-eye.

"No, no, silly," I said.

"Ladies and gentlemen, may I introduce to you Bajchem International, LLC! Can you tell what the company will do?"

"Sell chemicals, Mom," they all said in unison.

"What about BAJ? What do those letters stand for?"

With this question, they looked at me and rolled their eyes. It was obvious to them that BAJ was a combination of their initials.

"I am now the owner and founder of my very own company that will offer technical sales services to raw-materials suppliers in the global cosmetics industry," I exclaimed once the company was registered.

Everyone cheered. Even Mama, whom we all began referring to as Grandma, was beaming with pride; she jumped up and gave me a big hug and kiss.

This new venture would take me worldwide and hold me responsible for establishing revenues for multimillion-dollar corporations. Life was not just good; life was great.

The business did well for a while, but after nearly a decade of success in representing various notable suppliers in the industry and making headway in executing sales with a multitude of cosmetic manufacturers, I was not prepared to handle the avalanche of the 2008 national financial crisis. The business needed rescuing. Contracts were not being renewed; my head was spinning. My dream of being a successful entrepreneur was becoming foggy with uncertainty. Times were beginning to appear grim with pending defeat. The economy eventually went on a downward spiral, leading up to an unrelenting recession. The suppliers I connected with experienced a loss of revenue, which severely impacted Bajchem International's financial standing.

At that point, I had to sever my ties, dissolve the company, and reconsider my path going forward. It was time to reposition my career plans. Facing hard-knock times is a standard part of life; like most people across the nation, I was not spared. This time of my life gave true meaning to the proverbial saying "The higher you are, the harder you fall." But, instead of lowering my emotional resiliency, I wrestled with the problems. The harder I fought to stay afloat, the more catastrophic the situation became. I realized that this downward turn would require a long-term recovery effort.

Looking back, when I left Haiti, I faced one of the hardest challenges in my young life—learning to reinvent myself—and now, as an adult, this was somehow second nature to me. I did not grudgingly accept my fate to return to America just so I could fail. I came to overcome, and that's what my heart and mind were prepared to do. Still, my emotional well-being began to shift. My life was seemingly out of control, and worry was rampant in my mind. Would I be turning a dark corner?

My father had struggled with chronic health issues that contributed to his anxieties leading up to his final days. The thought crossed my mind that I might have my own struggles with which to deal. For the first time in a long while, I was consumed by all the events in my life. At that point, anxiety began to set in, and I felt it coming like a wave of deafening worry. When I finally woke up from a long, deep sleep, something shifted inside that led me to investigate who I was becoming. I had swallowed everything that was happening; there was no back door. I had to walk right through it.

Taking on a teacher role to educate myself about what was shaping my mind was the natural next step. This was my way of functioning—educating myself and using what I learned. My homeland of Haiti was a place where hope was a lost vision. I couldn't let my family down, and I wouldn't let failing shrink my core.

Months passed, and my best moving parts—mind and body—weakened even more. I remembered my father had his own way of dealing with his anxieties and kept it close as an example of what *not* to do. I sensed my mother's concern when she saw how weak I had become, sleeping throughout the day and remaining confined to one room within our home.

I didn't want to worry the kids. They were used to their mother being a mover and a shaker. So many years of climbing the hills of life had caught up with me. It was a complete invasion of mind, body, and soul. It was a loud cry for a physical and mental break.

First, a lifestyle change was obligatory. I learned that all consumption of stimulants like caffeine and depressants like alcohol had to end; I changed my diet to include healthier choices. I began a rigorous exercise routine of jogging, kickboxing, and Zumba classes. I learned how to practice mindfulness, indulged in warm baths, drank herbal tea, and listened to classical music. All the while, my children and mother surrounded me with support and encouragement.

After a few months, this slower pace and focus on my well-being began to show positive results. It was just a matter of time before I felt strong enough to shove myself out the door to explore my next career move. Handling finances had been my role for as long as I could remember, so getting a full-time job and finding new and exciting opportunities were on my agenda.

Browsing through the NYSCC newsletter's employment section, I found a position that piqued my interest, but would undoubtedly challenge my mind. The job requirements differed from my previous positions, but the customers would be the same. My level of interest was high because this role would require utilizing all the knowledge I had amassed from previous roles in raw-materials testing, formulating, quality control/quality assurance, and sales. Lo and behold, I needed to find my resume. Being a business owner, it had been a while since I had used one. A few updates needed to be done, and then it was sent. My heart was full of optimism.

The company was French, and that aligned perfectly with my background. I have always been lucky with French companies because of my unexpected French-language skills. School was in French for the first thirteen years of my life. I attended Mere Louise Elementary School established in Haiti by the Sisters of Saint Joseph of Cluny, a congregation founded by the Blessed Anne Marie Javouhey, who was born in Bourgogne, France, in the late seventeen hundreds. Though I am no longer fluent, I read and understand the French language very well.

Alas, a few weeks before receiving the call for the interview, I had foot surgery. Clearly, missing an interview was out of the question. But my only choice was to go on crutches. You can't make this stuff up.

How am I going to get there? Certainly, I cannot drive.

I called my childhood friend Donny, who now resides in Pennsylvania and was my neighbor back in Haiti in lakou dis pieces. "Donny, I was called for an interview. The job sounds very intriguing. My foot is in a cast, and I can't drive myself."

Well, Donny thought it was acceptable to show up in my disabled state. He offered to drive me. I hopped to his car on my crutches, and he helped me into the car. At first,

I thought he would encourage me to not go, but he just asked, "Are you going there to win it?"

I secretly knew that showing up on crutches was a bit unusual. The interviewer would either think I was profoundly weird or just plain unique. My answer to Donny's question was, however, "I will."

When I arrived at the office building, reality set in. After months of transitioning out of a rock-bottom position, I felt a bit loopy and inexperienced. But I proceeded to carefully hobble toward the receptionist.

"Good afternoon, I'm *Marie,* here to see Ms. Faro; I have a one o'clock appointment." Weariness had caught up with me after the walk from the car to the office, but I pretended to be put together.

"Yes, she will be ready for you in about five minutes," the receptionist responded politely as she eyed my crutches.

"Oh, this was a last-minute condition that I had to take care of. I thought of rescheduling, but you know how timing is everything."

"Sure, I get that," she said sympathetically, passing me a clipboard. "Please fill this out, and I'll let Ms. Faro know you're here."

"Thank you" was all I could say as I took hold of the clipboard, placed it under my armpit, and wobbled toward an available chair.

That's when I figured looking broken wouldn't give me points with my potential new employer. I wasn't too concerned, but I was nervous about offering my expertise in a field that was clearly in a different area of the cosmetics industry. But learning was my game, and I would chance it.

When Ms. Faro finally came out to greet me, her eyes looked at me with astonishment and awe. As if to say with her eyes, "Oh, poor you." At least, that's what I thought. The interview proceeded after I offered a short anecdote about my situation; then it closed with the customary "I'll let you know in a few days" ending.

I was hopeful because it was a French company, and I was very comfortable with the culture. However, in the end, they decided on another candidate.

One rejection prompted other doors to open. I worked on the job search and waited for the results. I needed to nurse my foot back to health since going on an interview with crutches may turn the scene into a *what-happened-to-your-foot* conversation, which wasn't the first impression I was going for.

Fully healed, I was lounging on the sofa, breathing in *fried plantains*,[17] compliments of Grandma's cooking in the nearby kitchen. Scanning the Internet for possible leads and checking my emails, I tilted my head when I saw a familiar name. To my amazement, it was Ms. Faro, the woman who had interviewed me a month before while I was on crutches. As it turned out, the person she hired didn't work out, and she wanted to know if I was still interested. I collected my thoughts, preparing for a professional comeback, and responded with controlled enthusiasm. I was definitely interested.

This upturn closed the gap between the ending of my company and the beginning of a new professional chapter. However, with the new position came technological requirements that would complement my repertoire of skills, so I needed to update my abilities. New challenges can boost creativity; I turned to my youngest daughter, a high school robotics team member.

"Jolia, guess what? I'm now selling software."

"Cool, Mom."

"Do you think I can do it?"

She broke out in a short laugh and a wide smile. "Sure. Why not?"

"But I think I'm going to need your help."

"Okay! Show me the system."

Her youthful and tech-savvy brain saved the day. My confidence was renewed.

If I've learned anything about life so far, a connected family can enhance growth for each other. With years of hand-holding parenting behind me—my girls were now in high school, and my son was in college—my children were learning how doing for your parent is a loving obligation.

They had seen my relationship with my mother for years—my taking care of her needs and her taking care of my kids. Everything worked to the advantage of the entire family. I found comfort in knowing this: our legacy was a continuity of love, support, and honor towards parents.

I was back on the road. *What is next?* I asked myself in the wee hours of the morning. I was a woman with an insatiable need to learn. I accepted the fact that the traditional roles assigned to women were not for me. I always strove for more—reaching into new frontiers, opening doors, and finding new opportunities would be my lifelong quest.

With my son in college, two daughters still in school, and my ever-supportive mother caring for us all, my family life was full of responsibilities and excitement. Everyone still depended on me to keep climbing up, one way or another. As I sat down for dinner, we talked about our week. The question came as to how I was managing my new job. It was one of those rare happy moments when everyone was on the same happiness level in their lives.

I then noticed a postcard nearby, standing out from the pile of mail on the kitchen counter. It was from Rutgers University. I quickly picked it up and read it. *Interesting. An MBA program. I felt butterflies in my stomach.* No words came out of my mouth this time, but something was planted in my mind. That night, I couldn't stop thinking about the description of the program on the postcard. More and more, going back to school once again was beginning to feel like the next logical move.

After a year under my belt at my new company, I was ready to spread my wings. The following week, I attended an information session about the program. I knew that earning additional educational credentials would add to my earning potential. By this time, I had been in the professional setting long enough to know that an MBA would lead my career upward. With nagging frustration, I suspected it would be an investment of time and money, both of which I was short of, but how could I say no to myself. How could I say no to my desire to learn?

I arranged a family meeting. Stirring the rice for the third time without serving anyone, I paused, put the large-sized spoon down on the counter, and it made a clanking noise. Jolia was relaxing on the couch, my son was sitting at the dining room table, and Ella was waiting to be called down from her room for dinner.

As I often did, I shouted out to summon them all together, "KIDS, let's talk. Come to the kitchen."

"Are we eating now?" My son was the first to respond.

"We'll eat soon, but I have something important to discuss. EL-LA, come down, please. Now!"

Then I motioned to Jolia to come to the dining area.

I stood by the counter in the kitchen, looking over at my firstborn, who was sitting patiently with his hands folded as if he were in school. Jolia sauntered over with a disinterested look on her face. They were about to hear my next mission, and I was hopeful that what I was about to say wouldn't take away from the family, but would add to it.

Ella finally came down and rushed to one of the dining room chairs, anxiously waiting to run back upstairs. Still waiting, my son was twiddling his thumbs, and Jolia rested her head on her fist with her elbow anchored to the table.

I circled around the counter to the refrigerator to get some water. I filled my glass, walked over to the table, and sat at the end. I knew I was procrastinating, but in my heart, this was another impending transition in all our lives.

"Kids, I need to share an idea with you."

"What?! Mom, stop being dramatic," my son jumped in. I could tell he wanted a quick-fix conversation.

"Well, I've been thinking of ways to improve my professional credentials, that is, and I have an idea." There—half of it left my mouth. It was unnerving to approach the conversation about my taking on another commitment that would cause a scheduling conflict, but I had to do it.

Jolia responded next, "Mom, are you thinking of changing your job or starting your business again? You had more time to be around when you did that."

Ella stayed quiet. She often took it all in and only spoke when she was ready to share her honest thoughts.

"It's like this—when you move up in the professional world, the more education you have, meaning your credentials, the more you are worth. And, of course, the more you actually know and the more you are worth, the more valuable you are. So I'm thinking about getting another master's degree, an MBA this time." Then I took a deep breath.

Ella responded immediately, "Mom, what exactly is an MBA?"

"I'm glad you asked. An MBA is a master's in business administration. Since it's an executive MBA that I'll pursue, it will be extremely fast-paced and requires a nearly two-year commitment. I'll have to work, too, so this will be challenging. Any other questions?"

By this time, there were three blank, neutral-looking faces staring back at me. Finally, my eldest spoke, "Mom, you should do it. That's a great plan."

Jolia spoke up next, "Going to get another master's is a good thing. More education puts you in with the competition."

She sounded years ahead of her age. *How does she know to think like that?* I thought.

"Yes, exactly, but I'll have to attend classes all day on Saturdays and meet with my team after work during the week. It's a huge commitment."

Ella was still quiet, but then she cleared her throat to announce her thoughts. "If you want to do it, just do it."

"One thing, though. I'm worried about Grandma. Ever since her diagnosis, she's been hard to handle," I added.

"Mom, don't worry. We can take care of Grandma. It's our turn now," my son jumped in. He was always the leader, which is often the case with the firstborn child. "Thinking about your future is a good thing."

Honestly, I was searching for a reason not to take on this new challenge, and relying on that reason to be the disruption it would cause my family. However, the discussion was working to my benefit. My mom wasn't part of the meeting just yet. I wanted to speak to the children first, then have her join us. We all knew she was dealing with dementia and might forget what was said. Still, I needed to talk to her and let her know my plan. I was holding on to who she used to be in my mind, which helped me manage my emotions.

"Jolia, go upstairs and get Grandma. I think she's finished with her nap." Now in her early nineties, Mom prefers to spend alone time in her room most days.

When everyone returned to the table, I turned and faced my mother. "Grandma, remember I mentioned that I'd like to learn more about the business world? Well, I was just talking to the kids about going for another degree."

"*TiFoune, TiFoune*, did you say you're going back to school for another degree?"

"Yes, Grandma."

"You know I will agree with your plans, no matter what. You always want to do better, so don't stop now. Yes, go for that degree and keep learning." She then got up and started clapping and dancing.

Then everyone joined in the happy dance. Through the years, my mother's tone has been the same—calm and knowing. This was all I needed to hear. Even with her new diagnosis, she was and always will be my greatest cheerleader.

With support from my mother and kids, I was cleared for takeoff. But I knew it would be a burden on all of us and especially on the kids, so I threw in a bonus. "Guess what, guys? There is one more thing. I'm getting a cleaning lady to help us around the house. It's important to keep this place organized and running smoothly. The priorities are to keep up with your studies as usual and watch over Grandma when she returns from the day care center, until the evening when the nurse arrives."

A chorus of "Yes!" was all I heard.

I wasn't sure if my family's enthusiasm was for the cleaning lady or me. Either way, they happily supported me. My plan to pursue this new endeavor was not only for me, but for my family, and it was my way of changing our legacy.

Now that my entire family knew of my plans, I began researching and applied to MBA programs at both Rutgers and Rider Universities, as a friend suggested. I met all the requirements and was accepted into both programs. Ultimately, I enrolled in the executive MBA program at Rider University.

I was grateful that my children, family, and friends respected my decision to invest the next two years in my educational goals. I felt more empowered than I ever had in my life. This educational experience would heighten my knowledge, and the executive MBA program would mold me into a resourceful businessperson. I was turning a corner that would impact my professional life.

By now, my son had graduated from Rutgers University, my alma mater, with degrees in history and economics. His brain came to the rescue with new knowledge when I felt immobilized by my studies. We sat at the kitchen table, the same one at which I hovered over him to help with his homework. He was now doing the same for me. Funnily, he played the role of the parent—*"You are not moving away from this table, young lady, until you fully grasp the material."* These tutorial sessions evoked a true dichotomy of emotions. I was annoyed, but beaming with pride. It was a mutual gain. This common bond—education—gave me the strength to keep going.

After seventeen grueling months fully immersed in all-day Saturday classes, case studies, nightly projects, presentations, and exams, I finally received a master's in business administration. Those three letters, MBA, will forever be associated with my name. I did wish my father were around to know about my latest success, but knowing that my children witnessed my newest achievement was enough. No more intense weeknights and weekends studying, isolating myself from friends, or denying life excursions that tempted me. Time and freedom were given back to me. So I thought!

The very last exam to complete my degree took place during the holiday season. How did we celebrate this milestone? We decided to throw the biggest New Year's Day party.

"This year, the celebration will have a casino theme complete with a blackjack table, slot machines and a dealer," I announced.

"Mom, can't we stick to our annual soup joumou,[18]as we always do on January 1?"

"No, no, my darling daughter, not this year. We took a chance, and we won big. Even Dessalines[19] would be pleased with us; we are winning at life."

"But, Mom, who's going to make the soup this year?"

"Well, Grandma, taught us well. Let's shave and peel all the vegetables, and my best friend will put it all together for us. In the meantime, we will pay close attention, so we can continue to uphold our Haiti's Independence Day tradition for years to come."

The party was well attended, and everyone brought their own dish from their own culture. We all consumed bowl after bowl of soup joumou, tasted each other's dishes, and had a cheerful time.

Sitting on the couch in the family room, scrolling through my Facebook feed after the party, I was still in celebratory mode. The graduation ceremony the previous week with the kids and Grandma was exhilarating.

Suddenly, a messenger notification caught my attention. The current treasurer of the New York Society of Cosmetic Chemists (NYSCC) had nominated me to be a candidate for the treasurer position. My eyes widened. The message also included a brief explanation about how having someone with an MBA on the executive board would be an asset to the chapter's mission of providing education to its members.

However, my vision of having any free time in the near future could suddenly vanish. Still, this was the next right move. The timing couldn't be more perfect or more aligned to where I was at that point in my life. I welcomed the opportunity to accept this professional nomination for a position within the largest chapter of the SCC. In the end, I was the elected candidate for a three-year term on the board. I soon discovered my inner direction and drive and allowed decisions to unfold, lead me, and coerce my inner passion for growth. NYSCC's executive board would become my next platform on which to learn and to give back.

In the meantime, the annual trade show hosted by the chapter was experiencing some growing pains, and European competitors were lurking to take control of the region. A fresh new leadership was indeed needed. My role as treasurer had barely ended when I was nominated to submit my candidacy for chair-elect of the chapter, thus assuming an additional three-year tenure on the board. Fear set in and rejected the nomination with a lengthy letter.

I secretly believed that I wasn't ready...or it wasn't the right choice...or worse, I didn't deserve or qualify for the nomination. I tried every excuse to get out of it. *What if I fail?* That thought chanted in my head. My confusion about worthiness stood post in my mind, but I had to change my belief rhythm and own what I'd worked so hard for. Dedication to my growth was who I was, and I wasn't going to let petty self-talk discourage or disparage me.

The realization of the lineup of all these events shook me inside, and I convinced myself to accept all that was happening. I was about to claim the role as the first person of African descent to chair the largest chapter of the NYSCC, a multimillion-dollar nonprofit organization, in its six-decade history. More importantly for me, I was the first Haitian to do so.

Where do I start? What is my vision for the upcoming year? How do I ensure that the annual trade show—which for many years has provided financial security for its members and is now on shaky grounds—remains with the chapter? These initial thoughts occupied my mind in the early days of accepting this huge responsibility. I desperately needed a pep talk from myself.

Just pretend this is a Harvard Business School case study, I thought to myself. From there on, the path became clear and straightforward. I needed to identify the problems and then develop a strategic plan to solve them. But, first, I needed a visual—a SWOT (strengths, weaknesses, opportunities, and threats) analysis.

First, the chapter had outgrown the space at the venue where the annual trade show was held. Additionally, a competitor was eager to establish itself as the premier trade show in North America. The board was aware of these threats, and panic set in, so I decided to utilize our *secret sauce—member loyalty to the organization's mission.* I knew the members' commitment was robust enough to overcome these formidable threats. Our weaknesses had to be corrected. Intelligence reports disclosed the opportunities within the industry, and the growth drivers were identified. This led to the development of the blueprint for a top-notch educational program aimed at equipping our members with knowledge of current market trends. The theme was sustainability, which included corporate social responsibility (CSR).

These platforms were carefully weaved into all the programs and were the driving factors in the year's success. The educational program was restructured to inform our members on upcoming trends to increase revenues in our market:

> **January:** *Eco Evolution.* Protect the planet, beginning with the ocean.

> **February:** *The Future of Sustainability.* Adopt a green business model to reduce our impact on the environment.

March: *Open Innovation.* Partner corporations with start-ups for business success.

April: *Globalization and Emerging Markets.* Focus on business beyond our shores—BRIC (Brazil, Russia, India, China, and South Africa) and Brexit (United Kingdom and European Union).

May: *NYSCC Suppliers' Day.* Multimillion-dollar trade show to launch latest innovations in materials and tools.

July: *91st ACS Colloid and Surface Science Symposium.* Exchange scientific information with American Chemical Society, the world's largest scientific organization and one of the world's leading sources of authoritative scientific information.

September: *#BeyondTheBrief.* The steps, beyond the marketing brief, to the launch of a new product.

October: *Innovations in Textured Hair Care.* Present technologies to address hair texture.

December: *Annual Education and Scholarship Award Ceremony.*

During the annual NYSCC Suppliers' Day trade show, science and beauty took center stage in New York City, and I was honored to lead the society in doing so. For the first time ever, the NYSCC Suppliers' Day was held at the world-renowned Jacob K. Javits Convention Center, a well-executed move. The show opened with a ribbon-cutting ceremony honoring all past chairs and executive board members of the chapter.

More than 400 exhibitors from sixty different countries came from around the world to promote their exclusive ingredients. Nearly 10,000 attendees arrived in the Hell's Kitchen section of Manhattan to find that unique ingredient to be incorporated into their new projects. That entire week during May of 2017, New York City was all about beauty.

On the showroom floor, various activities were offered. In the conference rooms notable speakers presented their latest research projects so that attendees could learn something new and exciting about personal care, hygiene, and beauty. Additionally, there were a hands-on workshop for future chemists and a corner to discover the pillars of sustainability. And close to my heart was the platform to explore the digital age of beauty, which was held in a theater, highlighting the benefits of technology in research and development as well as marketing. It was an overall massive trade show occupying more than 80,000 square feet. The event also hosted a spectacular award ceremony to recognize companies that successfully incorporated sustainability into their business models.

The chapter's mission includes outreach initiatives executed through scholarships and sponsorships. Thousands of dollars are donated annually to support scientific programs at universities and schools in the New York area. The aim is to create awareness of the cosmetics industry and to boost students' interest in careers in cosmetic science. Recipients of the scholarships are invited to the chapter's end-of-year award ceremony. It was my honor to select the recipients for the year. They included Fairleigh Dickinson University's School of Natural Sciences, Douglass College–Rutgers University (Advancing Women in STEM), Rider University's Living and Learning Community (Minor Science for Business), Rochester Institute of Technology–Golisano Institute for Sustainability, and Trenton Catholic Academy (Project Lead The Way Science Program).

The scholarship program extended beyond universities into high schools and middle schools with donations to PACE, You Be the Chemist, and Robbinsville High School's first robotics team. It was also the year of fostering greater unity among the chapters of the Society of Cosmetic Chemists and solidifying partnerships with organizations in the industry, including the International Federation of Society of Cosmetic Chemists (IFSCC), the national Society of Cosmetic Chemists, (SCC), Rodman Media, *Personal Care* magazine, the Personal Care Product Council (PCPC), Independent Cosmetic Manufacturers and Distributors (now Independent Beauty Association, or simply IBA), Cosmetic Executive Women (CEW), Peclers Paris, and FCE Cosmetique in Brazil.

Together with the board, we expanded our reach, disseminated scientific information to the public, and welcomed a new blogger! We established a scientific committee, a sponsorship committee, and a student mentorship committee to boost our educational program and communications with our members. We also launched a searchable database with a powerful search engine that would allow Suppliers' Day exhibiting companies to upload ingredient information they wished to promote at the upcoming show. In this way, it would encourage communication and interaction with show attendees before showtime.

The year 2017 was said to be one of the most successful years in the chapter's history, not just in revenues, but, more importantly, in innovative strategies implemented, newly established relationships with other industry organizations, and the level of engagement by the volunteers. It was also the year NYSCC's mission was prominently showcased on *Kathy Ireland Worldwide Business* on Bloomberg and Fox Business News Network.

In addition, arm in arm, volunteers, donors, and sponsors participated in a humanitarian effort and together planned a beauty-oriented mission project geared towards marginalized women. During Thanksgiving week, we successfully executed All About Beauty—a mission trip to the island of Haiti to introduce basic cosmetic science to women in the region. The aim was to empower local women by giving them a new door to walk through. This project was about teaching and encouraging women, who otherwise would be subjected to a lifetime of being a home-maker or local fruit-and-vegetable vendor, to start a business by making basic cosmetics products using local natural ingredients and raw materials from the United States.

This beauty event included a full day of glamour and beauty, followed by a photo shoot for the women who participated in the program. The event was designed with a greater emphasis on making the women feel pampered and beautiful, if only for one day. It gave us great satisfaction that the women were eager to learn a new skill that could change their lives forever. Even though hardship weighed them down—and the sacrifice was great they had to make to give us a few days of their lives—they still showed up ready to take on this adventurous journey. Permeating the air was their heightened self-esteem and exceptional pride.

Women and children typically come as a package. So we included a session for the kids. We felt a STEM project, if planned carefully, could drop seeds of greatness in each child's mind. More importantly, the project would have to be fun. My daughter Jolia, who spent her years in high school on a robotics team, was the perfect candidate to lead this project. To our great surprise, her team gleefully jumped on board. Team Nemesis FRC2590 International Outreach was launched to support our endeavor. Based on the sheer number of LEGOs collected, it is possible that every parent in the town of Robbinsville in Mercer County, New Jersey, participated in the drive. Students and mentors used their expertise in CAD (computer-aided design) to create a challenge for the kids, which would ultimately lead to the creation of a robot.

When the children completed the challenge, the smiles on their faces revealed their contentment in knowing they, too, could learn if afforded the opportunity. This initiative to empower women and children, one country at a time, could not have taken off without a network of support. Communities, schools, family members, friends, and many industry companies supported this call to action with their willingness to participate and provide supplies, gifts, and sponsorships to make it all happen. To identify and collaborate with people in the industry *and* community—people sharing a sense of social responsibility and willing to share their time, money, and skills—was priceless.

Chapter 14
The Family's Circle of Dreams Moves Forward

Family means the world to me, and I yearned for the family that I left behind in Haiti at thirteen. But if I couldn't relive the past, I would live for the future and create my own loving family. Reflecting on my life, I believe that I designed what I envisioned in my heart.

My firstborn and only son lived off the loving kindness of both my mother and me in his growing years. Like most single parents, I doted on him and supplied him with extra doses of care and attention. I think we spoiled him to help ease the pain of the separation from his father at an early age. In turn, he sported a dynamic personality from all this attention. His endearing looks were an added bonus. People were drawn to his dark-brown, prominent, round eyes, long eye lashes, and radiant smile (compliments of his grandma), so he never fell short on stealing the show.

His kindergarten teacher once said, "This is the most mature kindergartner that I've ever had in my class. We have the most interesting conversations!"

However, my son sometimes showed shades of sensitivity, shedding tears from time to time, transforming from an astute man-child into a vulnerable, age-appropriate young boy. To this day, he has a full spectrum of emotions that he shares without restraint.

Throughout his growth years, we traveled around the United States and abroad. This exposed him to cultures far removed from his familiar surroundings. From all his travels, he has become a connoisseur of all things fine and good. Once, he was a sports ambassador with People to People, an organization founded by President Eisenhower; it connects children from all nations. When sports entered his world, he traveled to the UK, Germany, and Italy for soccer tournaments; these opportunities made him an open-minded, enthusiastic person who thirsted for more life experiences. I wore the soccer-mom hat and escorted him to game after game, from state to state, until he discovered the next sport. And the next one. And the next. He championed each sport, whether it was football, golf, karate, or skating. Always the consummate athlete, he still holds true to his physical form today.

He graduated from my old alma mater, Rutgers University, and then sailed off to begin a career in New York with an investment firm. Corporate America seduced him. My motherly eyes twinkled with pride when he arose at dawn to catch NJ Transit to New York City—the same transportation system his grandfather Joe, my dad, began working at decades ago. A world apart, but connected.

"Honey, the coffee is on," I yelled when I heard his footsteps.

"Thanks, Mom!" he shouted back.

He longed for a connection to his culture and country, the beloved country that I left, so he independently sought out a plan to visit Haiti. He traveled with a group of investment bankers whose mission it was to join humanitarian forces to build much-needed schools and hospitals in the Grand Bois[20] region. While there, my son Skyped with me and gave me a virtual tour of the tiny forgotten island where I was born.

"Mom, I'm here in this glorious land! This beautiful land that we should've come to together."

"You know my thinking. I would have loved to."

I didn't respond in detail because we talked about visiting Haiti in circles. When the topic came up, I told my kids that I carried a lot of fear about going back; I no longer had any family members there. My brother Yves-Antoine I left in Haiti took some time off from his job at the sugar company to visit us in the United States. From there, he visited his first girlfriend in Montreal and got married. With the constant political strife and civil unrest, it wasn't always a good environment in which to spend our summer vacations.

There were certainly memories dressed with joyous family occasions and the raw laughter of friends, but there was also a darkness that I wasn't ready to face. I did my part by changing the course of our family's educational road map. I think the next generation—my children—can change the rest.

Amazingly, my son soon learned to master the French Creole language in loyalty to his ancestral roots. I learned that he seized every opportunity to practice with his grandma. He also had cousins in France, Canada, and Haiti who welcomed speaking the customary language with him. He embraced everything about his background. Again, I stood proud.

As life happens, he networked his way into an interview in Miami, Florida. I dropped him at the airport, cheered him off with a massive hug and affectionate double kisses on his handsome cheeks, and wished him, "Great luck!"

A phone call later turned into "I've got the job! I'm staying in Miami!"

Wanting your child to succeed is one thing, but having them depart abruptly from your motherly range leaves a void I can't explain.

"Mom, please ship my dress shirts to my dad's house. I will stay there until I find a place near the financial district."

So life as we know it began for him. Then California was his next destination, which is where he is today.

Out of Haiti came a little girl whose dream was unknown, but planned by her elders. In this sense, my eldest son and his sisters will also seed growth in their Haitian families, as I did for them. The family circle of dreams moves forward.

Epilogue
Coming Home

Decades ago, I left my homeland of Haiti as a thirteen-year-old and in a quandary of thoughts occupied with misgivings and uneasiness, not to mention a ton of fear; I was headed to the Land of the Free—the United States of America. It is no coincidence that the plaque at the base of the Statue of Liberty reads, "Give me your tired, your poor, your huddled masses yearning to breathe free, the wretched refuse of your teeming shore. Send these, the homeless, tempest-tossed to me; I lift my lamp beside the golden door!"

The mission began with my father and mother chaperoning my future in ways I could never repay. How can you measure support, guidance, and love for the next generation...and the next? Today I stand proud of all that was shaped for me, no matter the sacrifices.

Living in America made me realize whom I had the potential to become, where I came from, and the elements needed to achieve stability and success. So my final mission was to return to Haiti and support those who continue to hope and dream for more, just as I did. If leaving Haiti was an emotional challenge, returning to Haiti doubled in emotion, but of a different kind. I was embraced by exhilaration and jubilation when I began planning a trip back to Haiti; it had been a long time coming.

Beware of opportunities; they come as unexpected as winning a lottery. The trade show at the Mandalay Bay in Las Vegas, Nevada, which I attend each year, was predictably exhausting, yet exhilarating. Sauntering down the aisles and conversing with other professionals and prospects was my role for that week, and I loved every minute of it. I think I was born for it! I must confess that is when I am at my best, when my light shines the brightest.

My career path as a professional cosmetic chemist, sharp businesswoman, and the 2017 chair of the board of NYSCC aligned with one of my missions in life—to be a self-assured, educated professional paving my own way. Outwardly, I was wrapped in self-satisfaction that day. My dedication to my career was evident, but an aching, unvoiced desire in my bones guided my thoughts, on that frenetic day, toward merging my professional life with my personal history.

My children were exploring their individual paths through their own educational and professional pursuits, which left me immensely content. After all, my parents' dream that I surpass them became a reality while they were still alive, and now I was witnessing the next generation, my children, take full advantage of continuing on a successful path. With each passing decade since I arrived in America, I strived to seize any educational opportunity for the sake of proving the worthiness of my parents' decision for me to leave Haiti at the tender age of thirteen. Through all the setbacks and successes, I believed it was all for good. Patience and open-mindedness led me to each next phase.

This time, unexpectedly, another next phase appeared faithfully right under my nose. Eyeing a seat from afar, I noticed an empty spot next to an equally exhausted-looking woman. I began walking fast despite my aching feet and approached the seat before anyone could claim it. As if it were with my last breath, I remarked, "Do you mind if I sit here?"

In her polite Southern accent, she offered a "not at all" response as she moved over on the bench.

Our conversation continued as if we were a couple of old friends. We shared our excitement about navigating such a massive show floor and complained about our hurting feet. Before long, she confided in me that she had been taking care of a sick family member, and her personal responsibilities had kept her from ever attending the show before. Eventually, names were exchanged along with business cards.

I instantly felt that this chance encounter meant something more. Fifteen minutes later, I was spilling thoughts about my longing to discover my legacy. With my mother not well—the dementia was ever present—and my children spreading their wings and leaving the home nest, my heart was searching for my life's meaning and purpose. Sharing personal information is not something I usually do—I'm still a reserved Haitian—but the time, place, and person felt comfortable.

Melle, my chance-encounter friend, continued to chat about the trade show, her brand, and how steaming-hot Las Vegas weather was. Then she mentioned a former coworker whose mission trip to Haiti was coming up in the fall; she was planning to join. Her coworker's lifelong dream was to help impoverished children and families in Haiti.

My ears perked up, and my chest beat with curiosity as I caught her gaze and responded, "That's so interesting! Haiti is my birthplace. When I was only thirteen, my mother sent me to America to live with my father."

She tilted her head with equal curiosity and asked me a few questions about how it felt to leave Haiti, whether I still had family there, and if I had been back since I left.

Bells rang in my head. I began to think that this chance conversation was connecting me to my legacy. *This is it. This means something. Right here, right now, something is being presented to me, so I better listen carefully.*

"Melle, please tell me more about your friend in Haiti and her mission."

The conversation continued, and my mind was spinning again. But, shortly, I had to get back to work. We said goodbye and promised to stay in touch. That happenstance meeting led me to reach out to her former coworker, who was pioneering a mission to Haiti to help children, and the community at large, who were born into chronic poverty. She has since founded a life-altering nonprofit organization to serve the people in Haiti. They provide resources to orphaned children, many of whom have living parents who cannot care for their own families. Sadly, Haiti is home to hundreds of thousands of orphans; parents who are trapped by generational poverty give up their rights in hopes that their children will receive the basics—food, shelter, health care, and education. The mission focuses on building stronger communities and families through sustainable education programs and orphan care.

This narrative was intimately familiar to me. I, too, was a child whose parents decided to relinquish maternal custody so my life could be better. I was instantly committed to their mission, and it didn't take long to decide that *I was going back to Haiti*. I needed to fuse the gap between my American life and my Haitian roots. Even more so, I wanted to help in whatever possible way that I could. The timing was right to return to Haiti, and I was prepared emotionally, economically, and educationally. My professional credentials and motivational mindset were at their peak. Reaching out to others who needed inspiration, education, and other means of help was my planned mission, my next stage. I was prepared to offer what I could, and the timing was right to give back. How could I forget where I came from?

Sharing my plan to return to Haiti with my family members heightened the emotions of the upcoming Thanksgiving holiday season. After more than four decades of being away, I would step foot on my native land, and my youngest daughter would join me in all of my glory and experience her mother's full circle.

During those weeks preparing for my trip, the anticipation of returning to my homeland with a sense of giving back filled my heart and soul with a deeper love for Haiti. The week prior, I was in a scrambling state of mind, trying to fulfill the needs of the mission, gathering donations, educational and medical supplies, clothing, and other items for the children in the orphanage. I was in a state of healthy anxiety.

The day arrived. Jolia and my good friend Meena joined Melle and me on this adventure. We called ourselves the Fabulous Four. Sitting on the plane, daydreaming about nothing in particular, I tried to act as if my trip back to Haiti was like any other everyday excursion. Through work, I have become a world traveler, but this wasn't a casual trip. Haiti, the country where my mother and father gave me my start in life, was where my character formed roots—solid, resilient, and powerful—and made me the woman I am today.

My only wish was for my mother, my anchor, to be beside me, but her health condition was an issue. Thinking about how this trip would have been enhanced with her by my side, I dozed off. Then disturbing turbulence caused a commotion on the plane that woke me up and raised my anxiety level. I opened my eyes to the sound of passengers praying loudly and others screaming.

I heard my friend Meena shout, "The pilot did say there would be a little turbulence, and there is nothing to worry about! Why are you all screaming?"

Then the turbulence stopped, and the flight attendant began to playfully tease the passengers. I turned and checked on Jolia, and she was still comfortably asleep. Soon, my emotions stabilized. I was ready to see my darling Haiti, the Pearl of the Antilles.

When I stepped off the plane, I felt simmering emotions welling up inside, but I kept them under control. Jolia grinned about the ruckus on the plane and the slight anxiety she sensed I was projecting. She then held my hand. She, too, was embarking on her own unique journey to sow the seeds of greatness among the young generation in her mother's homeland. Collaborating with her high school's robotics team, her mission involved paving the way for engineering concepts in the minds of children. Stressing the importance of STEM, she often says, "For Haiti to transform, the children must learn how to build."

This moment in time, sharing this experience with her, warmed my insides.

I turned around to witness the scenery, the aroma, the people, and the almost familiar place I had left long ago. What I saw didn't resemble a past that I knew; it was now a country that I had detached from as part of the immigrant's natural experience. My American roots were deeper in some ways—by default, that is—but Haiti still had roots in my soul. It was indisputable that the blessings in my lifetime were countless, and being in Haiti that Thanksgiving week made me even more grateful for my life after my departure from my homeland. My favorite quote crossed my mind: "From everyone to whom much has been given, much will be required; and from the one to whom much has been entrusted, even more will be demanded."

My heart was entranced by the sweet whisper of the drums calling me from the mountains, signaling my next steps. I listened, and I began moving to the rhythm of the Kompa, finding my way to make a difference in this world. I then realized that the proper way to say thank you is to give back. As founder of Itiah Angels for Learning, I believe that I am on my way.

Footnotes

[1] *TiFoune:* Marie's nickname used by family and close friends.

[2] *Trouin:* A town in the Arrondissement of Léogâne located southwest of Port-Au-Prince, the capital of Haiti.

[3] *Chansonettes françaises:* French songs.

[4] *Rest avek:* Living with. A practice of sending children to live with someone else.

[5] *Lakou dis pieces:* A ten-room community rowhouse; each room is rented out to a different family.

[6] *Raconteurs:* Storytellers.

[7] *Certificat:* A mandatory exam that students must pass to certify the completion of their primary education. Passing it is required for students to continue their education into secondary education.

[8] *Camionette:* Small pickup truck designed to use as a taxi. Usually highly decorated and painted many colors.

[9] *Tassot*: Goat meat marinated overnight, cooked with spices, and then fried.

[10] *Pate tomate*: Tomate paste.

[11] *Frites*: French fries.

[12] *Tap tap*: Another name for the camionettes.

[13] *Chaudière*: Deep pan, with a long handle, used for boiling or stewing food.

[14] *Fourneaux*: Cooking stove.

[15] *Mulats*: Mulattoes. *People of mixed race, White and Black.*

[16] *Kompa*: A genre of Haitian music and dance.

[17] *Fried plantains:* Also known as tostones.

[18] *Soup joumou*: A soup made of squash, vegetables, and meat. Haitians and everyone of Haitian descent eat this on New Year's Day to celebrate Haiti's Independence Day of January 1, 1804.

[19] *Dessalines*: The first president of Haiti. He was the general who led the revolution against Napoleon's army, liberating Haiti from slavery.

[20] *Grand Bois*: A region in the West Department of Haiti, located near the border of the Dominican Republic.

www.ingramcontent.com/pod-product-compliance
Lightning Source LLC
LaVergne TN
LVHW021447080426
835509LV00018B/2194